PLIGHT OF INDIAN FARMER AND AGRICULTURE

VIJAY PAL SINGH TONK

BlueRose ONE.com
Stories Matter
NewDelhi • London

BLUEROSE PUBLISHERS
India | U.K.

BlueRose ONE
Stories Matter
New Delhi • London

For permissions requests or inquiries regarding this publication, please contact:

BLUEROSE PUBLISHERS
www.BlueRoseONE.com
info@bluerosepublishers.com
+91 8882 898 898
+4407342408967

ISBN: 978-93-6783-898-3

Cover Design: Shubham
Typesetting: Sagar

First Edition: January 2025

I am not reputed as a charismatic leader with a gifted pen; a youthful firebrand, at once impassioned and refined. But I begin fitfully to work on a sequel. This is due to vast erudition and cognizant knowledge invariably delighted me to pen down the facts on farmers, poor people and labour class in our country. This memoir is interleaved with political and social commentary of agrarians and poor proletariats, and all this is contained with in the narrative that spans Indian history from the Indus Valley up to present time. It is an act of my political Social, and literary imagination.

This sequel delves deep with the sources of India's national peasantry. Peasantry always sequestered from rest of the world. Poor and proletariat people are also deprived of all basic to needs. My poor will persuade you to ponder on a unique array of their culture, religion and ways of living.

This sequel contains the delightful pen and ink work of that master of illustration.

Agriculture has remained a traditional forte of developing economics for a long time. Our economy is based on agriculture. Agriculture is, we can say, a backbone of our nation and its development.

Our country India is rich in all natural elements. From Kashmir to Kanya Kumari and from Gujrat to Assam, scores of natural resources and fertility of land are embedded in her heart. Apart from her high fertility, her class of peasantry and labourers still have to face the music in their day-to-day life. If a farmer is not able to fill his belly, how can he be able to feed others? If a labourer does not have any basic needs or requirements for his survival fulfilled, how can he build a nation?

Unfortunately, these helping hands of our society, and our nation are still deprived of many basic needs ranging from food to shelter, from ropes to medical treatment. No hand comes forward for their help. Only some false statements are made by the politicians and arrest the desires of these people. But these poor people play with the polarities between and within the two bluff masters: politicians and the elite class of the nation.

Poverty is a disease and economic liberalization is a cure. The measure is directed towards giving a boost to the economy which lies in the doldrums even after half a century of achieving independence and to divert from the hackneyed socialist approach which has failed to meet its prime objective of eradicating poverty. Poverty lies in every nook and corner of our society.

But does anyone think about where this poverty sprouted and how? In short, poverty is the result of poor peasantry. I'll try to illuminate this point in my text. I'll try to elucidate my view on the plight of farmers and poor people and their remedies.

Indeed, an honest and objective approach to the people's problems can make a difference in the quality of governance. What we need is a work culture and certain values, rather than dogmas that can help us address today's wayward traits in the polity. Corruption and nepotism must be eradicated from the society, or they will eat into its social fabric. Dogmas should be fashioned and implemented on prodigious scale.

As such, we think that there is nothing we can do about poverty. Lack of political will to tackle it is the main cause of poverty in our country. Imparting practical education might be the right step. The solution is clear: poverty has to be tackled with sound economic programs. What we need is a management commission, not a planning commission.

Even before independence, some Britishers, who continue to offer advice, warned that agriculture must not be neglected and should have the first priority. Only a person with minimal intelligence can ignore or neglect agriculture or forget the peasant. The Indian peasant, more than anyone else, is the key to India's progress. But our crisis in agriculture, grave as it is, is interlinked with the crisis in industry, from which it arose. The two cannot be disconnected and dealt with separately. It is essential to address the disproportion between the two to be remedied.

There was a time when our farmers were made serf by the British. Their policies were rigid and led to plight of farmers. Our farmers were deprived of their land and reduced to labour class, becoming homeless and wandering to meet their end.

After independence, due to education, just few years back, a change has come. The Green revolution has brought a dynamic shift in agriculture. Today agriculture is not merely just farming;

it has become a complete industry. A farmer has progressed and moved into other fields of development.

But, despite this progress, our farmers and other labour classes are still at the mercy of fate. An uncharted sea full of challenges still lies ahead. Now new problems are emerging. We must gird up our loins and sharpen our wits to face the challenge, such as poverty, and uplift the farmer by providing good education and support.

Luculcate moral values in the child at the time he can cotton on, all things, so that he may help others when he'll grow and build the strong nation.

Seven social sins enunciated by Mahatma Gandhi are:-

1. Politics without principles.
2. Wealth without work.
3. Pleasure without conscience.
4. Knowledge without character.
5. Commerce without morality.
6. Science without humanity.
7. Worship without sacrifice.

We must follow human values for the betterment of mankind. A child of today must become a master of future- whether in field or in science. He'll fashion the nation. A child may be a farmer, but a farmer can produce highbrows from himself. Examples you'll find in the leaves of sequel go ahead.

There have always been two different world, two different nations since the very beginning of society. There are always two ideologies, two different paths, and two different social lives and these differences still persist. They are like two poles of Earth. Just as the two poles can't come together, these two different world cannot merge. The poor and the rich, the peasant and the elite, representing two different facets of life, and they are tough to amalgamate.

Discrimination and segregation are rampant. Corruption and nepotism are widespread in our society poisoning our development. What name should we give this society- an ersatz society? In such an atmosphere, our nation will not last long. Sooner or later, our social edifice will be dilapidated. And if the social fabric of our society tears apart, what will our nation be called? A nation stripped of its culture and unity? The development of the nation will stunted.

For the betterment of the nation, the hands of the peasantry, labour, and capitalists must join together.

So come forward with an open heart to help poor people of our country. Try to uplift poor peasants and labourers by accepting them as your own blood. There is one most important element in our body that make us live, that make us breathe, and that is our soul. Soul is the embodiment of God. God is everywhere. He dwells in every being. Every human being is a member of His family. If we all are His part, all are His family members, than how can we be segregated from each other on the basis of caste, creed or religion? Segregated for food and wealth? There are many problems to discuss, but most pressing, I think, is the miserable condition of Indian peasant and poor labourers. Farmers produce food but are deprived of food himself; labourers build skyscrapers but rest on pavements. An ugly picture of modernization, or an irony of fate.

Today, the government is also taxing agriculture land in possession for the sake of nation's economic development. Wealthy businessmen purchase fertile land from farmers at high prices in return. The government accompanies these people in some spheres. But ch....... (page 8) on this malpractising. Agricultural land will soon be depleted if the acquisition of land does not cease. If land is required for construction, barren or less fertile land should be used for the purpose.

Once again, the same situation has erupted for farmers as it did in pre-independence era. Poor farmers are gradually becoming landless. Again, they are sailing (page 8) in the same boat in which they once anchored.

No situation has changed for farmers or labourers since the existence of society or the nation. Let us scrutinize the entire picture and the contour of this facet of life, and try to understand whether God weeps or not.

In India, by contrast, extraordinary freedom and flexibility of the mind have persistently juxtaposed with the most rigid social structures, resulting in a curious combination of conservatism in practice and explosive thought. The Indian mind has now taken a flight, while the Indian social order remains a prison. So, why can't these two different worlds—of the poor and the rich, of farmers and landlords—be juxtaposed into one. The amalgamation of different societies is required for the everlasting prosperity of mankind.

'RYOT'

On the heart of land,
He shows the work of the land,
From cockcrow to twilight,
With many troubles he has to fight.

He is always in busy toil,
But never found in loll,
Hurrying to do and hurry to gain,
But unluckily, he fails.

In the fields of the state,
The Ryot is there, playing with his fate;
He is a benefactor and distributes grain,
But, as you know, he never himself gains.

He is simple 'nd happy with his lot,
But the haves are still poor,
Because they are not contented with their lots,
So he makes hay for these poor.

He has lost his youth, for the gloomy hope,
His playmates are sickle, plough, 'nd rope;
His youth is for others, not for himself,
His desires are shattered 'nd trampled
For others, but never fulfilled for himself.

So we must pay heed to the development of farmers and labourers. Come and join together for the upliftment of these two trampled societies in our country. Remove all barricades from their way and guide them to their goal. A goal full of gaiety and prosperity. Give them a full and proper space to breathe in and expand their vigour. They will expand nation. I am sure.

Today, as the energies of new generations romanticise our country, it is more important than ever to re-examine the founding texts of modern India. We must ask new questions of them, read them against the grain, and test their resources in the face of new dilemmas. Equality, though, we should test the new principles we might wish to arrest, the new ideas we seek to realize, against the truths and wagers of our founding vision. In the task of maintaining democracy, we must juxtapose all different societies into a single and powerful nation; a strong nation build by labourers and fed by peasants.

They are the sons of the soil; don't deprive them of their motherland. They are assets of our nation. Don't eliminate them; fuel them with love, care, and values. We must be provident by making these class provident.

"Well begun is half done" is my attempt at work for the peasant.

Today's plight of these poor people is the result of our one-sided theory of development. The economic and industrial revolutions, simultaneously and rapidly, eroded the farmers' land and left them at a low ebb forever.

I want to elucidate the above-mentioned lives within the vast history created by British before independence in our country.

As you all know, we, the people of India, were ruled by British for last two hundred years. They ruled us with a divide-and-rule policy. They trampled our people, our dignity, our work, our jobs, looted us of our wealth, and left us at a low ebb forever. Now a question arises... How? How?... and How? How did our civil organization came to an end? During British Raj, the regime of our country was stagnant for a long time.

The East India Company arrived in our country during the reign of Mughal king Jahangir in 1600 BC. The company de-boarded at licut-beach. The moment British company stepped onto the holy shores of our land, the ill fate commenced, proving to be ominous for India.

The chief business of the East India Company in its early period, the very object for which it was started, was to carry Indian manufactured goods, textiles, etc., as well as spices and the like from the East to Europe, where there was a great demand for these articles. With the development in industrial techniques in England, a new class of industrial capitalists rose there, demanding a change in this policy. The British market was to be closed to Indian products, and the Indian market was to be opened to British manufactures. The British parliament, influenced by this new class, began to take a greater interest in India and the working of the East India Company.

To begin with, Indian goods were excluded from Britain by legislation, and as East India Company held a monopoly in the India export business, this exclusion influenced other foreign markets also. This was followed by vigorous attempts to restrict and crush Indian manufacturing through various measures and internal duties that prevented the flow of Indian goods within the country itself. British goods, meanwhile, had free entry. The

Indian textile industry collapsed, affecting vast numbers of weavers and artisans. The process was rapid in Bengal and Bihar, elsewhere it spread gradually with the expansion of British rule and the building of railways. It continued throughout the nineteenth century, breaking up other old industries as well—shipbuilding, metalworking, glass, paper, and many crafts.

To some extent, this was inevitable as the old manufacturing came into conflict with the new industrial technique. But it was hastened by political and economic pressure, and no attempt was made to apply the new techniques to India. Indeed every attempt was made to prevent this happening, and thus the economic development of India was arrested, and the growth of the new industry prevented. Machinery could not be imported into India. A vacuum was created, which could only be filled by British goods, leading to rapidly increasing unemployment and poverty. The classic type of modern colonial economy was built, with India becoming an agricultural colony of industrial England, supplying raw materials and providing markets for England's industrial goods.

The liquidation of the artisan class led to unemployment on a massive scale. What were all these millions, who had so far been engaged in industry and manufacture, to do now? Where were they to go? Their old profession was no longer open to them, and the way to a new one was barred. They could die of course; that way of escape from an intolerable situation is always open. They did die in tens of millions. The English Governor-General of India, Lord Bentinck, reported in 1834 that "the misery hardly finds a parallel in the history of commerce. The bones of the cotton weavers are bleaching the plains of India."

But still vast numbers of them remained, and these increased from year to year as British policy affected more remote areas of the country and created more unemployment. All these lords of artisans and craftsmen had no job, no work, and all their ancient skills was useless. They drifted to the land, for the land was still there. But the land was fully occupied and could not possibly absorb them profitably. So, they became a burden on the land, and the burden grew. With it grew the poverty of the country, and the standard of living fell to incredibly low levels. This compulsory back-to-the-land movement of artisans and craftsmen led to an ever-growing disproportion between agriculture and industry. Agriculture became more and more the sole business of the people due to the lack of occupations and wealth-producing activities.

India became progressively ruralized. In every progressive country, there has been, during the past century, a shift of population from agriculture to industry, from village to town. In India, this process was reversed as a result of British policy. The figures are instructive and significant. In the middle of the 19th century, about 55% of the population is solid to have been dependent on agriculture; secondly, this proportion was estimated to be 74% (this was pre-war figure). Though there has been greater industrial employment during the war, the number of those dependent on agriculture actually went up in the census of 1941 owing to increase of population. The growth of a few large cities (chiefly at the expense of the small town) is apt to mislead the superficial observer and give him false idea of Indian conditions.

This, then, is the real, the fundamental cause of the appalling poverty of the Indian people, and it is of comparatively recent origin. Other causes that contributing to it are themselves the result of this poverty, chronic starvation, undernourishment, and issues like disease and illiteracy. Excessive population is unfortunate, and steps should be taken to curb it wherever necessary, but it still compares fanousably (page 16) with the density of population of many industrialized countries. It is only excessive for a predominately agricultural community, and under a proper economic system, the entire population can be made productive and should all to the wealth of the country. As a matter of fact, great density of population exists only in special area like Bengal and Gangetic valley, while vast areas are still sparsely populated. It is worth remembering that Great Britain is more than twice as densely populated as India.

The crisis in industry spread rapidly to the land and became a permanent crisis in agriculture. Holdings became smaller and smaller, and fragmentation proceeded to an absurd and fantastic degree. The burden of agricultural debt grew, and ownership of the land often passed to moneylenders. The number of landless labourers increased by the millions. India was under an industrial-capitalist regime, but her economy was largely that of the pre-capitalist period, minus many of the wealth-producing elements of that pre-capitalist economy. She became a passive agent of modern industrial capitalism, suffering all tis ills and with hardly any of its advantages.

The transition from a pre-industrialist economy to a capitalist industrialization economy involves great hardship and heavy cast in human suffering borne by masses. This was especially true in the early days when no efforts were made to plan the transition or to lessen its harmful results, leaving everything to individual initiative. There was hardship in England during this period, but overall, it was not severe because the changeover was rapid, and the unemployment caused was soon absorbed by new industries.

However, that does not mean that the cost in human suffering was not paid. It was indeed paid, and paid in full by others, particularly the people of India, through famine, death, and vast unemployment. A significant portion of the costs of transition to industrialism in Western Europe were paid for by India, China, and other colonial countries, whose economies were dominated by European powers.

It is obvious that there has been all along abundant material in India for industrial development managerial and technical ability, skilled workers even some capital in spite the continuous drain from India. The historian, Montgomery Martin, giving evidence before an enquiry committee of the British parliament in 1840, stated: "India is as much a manufacturing country as an agricultural one; and he who would seek to reduce her to the position of an agricultural country seeks to lower her in the scale of civilization." That is exactly what the British sought to do in India, continuously and persistently. The measure of their success is the present condition of India, after they have hold despotic sway there for a century and a half. Ever since the demand for the development of modern industry arose, which I imagine was at least 140 years ago, we have been told that India is pre-eminently an agricultural country, and it is in her interest to stick to agriculture. Industrial development might upset the balance and prove harmful to her main business agriculture. The solicitude which British industrialist and economists have shone for the India peasant has been truly gratifying. In view of this, and the tender care lavished upon him by the British Government in India, one can only conclude that some powerful and malign fate, some supernatural force, has countered their intentions and measures, making the peasant one of the poorest and most miserable being on earth.

It is now difficult for anyone to oppose industrial development in India, but even today, when any extensive and far-reaching plan is proposed, we are warned by our British friends, who continue to shower their advice upon us, that agriculture must not be neglected and must take precedence. As if any Indian with an iota of intelligence can ignore or neglect agriculture or forget the peasant. The Indian peasant is India more than anyone else, and it is on his progress that India's progress depends upon. But our crisis in agriculture, as grave as it is, is interlinked with the crisis in industry, out of which it arose. The two cannot be disconnected and dealt with separately, and it is essential for the disproportion between the two to be remedied.

Long subjection of a people and the denial of freedom bring many evils, and perhaps the greatest of these lies in the spiritual sphere: demoralization and the sapping of the people's spirit. It is hard to massive this, thought it may be obvious. It is easier to trace and measure the economic decay of a nation, and as we look back on British economic policy in India, poverty is the ineluctable consequence of it. There is no mystery about this poverty; we can see the causes and follow the process which have led to the present condition.

India's farming population has decreased by nine million in last ten years. Census 2011 data, released on April 30, 2013, showed that the number of farmers in India has fallen by 9 million over the last decade. While the ratio of farmers to the country's total workforce has been diminishing steadily for some time, this is the first time since 1974 that the size of the farming population has declined in absolute terms.

The Census data divides the total workforce into four industrial categories: cultivators, agricultural labourers, household industry workers and others. While 'others' remain the largest group, cultivators also have a considerable portion of the total workforce numbering 119 million. Cultivators, however, now constitute less than a quarter of the total workforce, representing a decline of several percentage points since the 2001 census.

Over the last half-century, the proportion of farmers to the country's total population had been falling in a steady manner. But the fall had not been large enough to result in a decline in absolute numbers. In the last decade, however, the decline in farming, combined with a slowing rate of population growth, has led to a decrease in the absolute number of farmers in the country.

As in previous decades, the proportion of agriculture labour has scaled up during the last decade as well. Experts say that the rise in agricultural labour can be explained by the decreasing size of land holdings over time.

Now I am stepping ahead with a problem related to the above or we can say coming out of it. It's a poverty.

Very well said by Nelson Mandela,

"Overcoming poverty is not a task of charity; it is an act of justice. Like slavery and apartheid, poverty is not natural. It is man-made, and it can be overcome."

Poverty takes birth from unemployment, landless farmers, and injustice.

It is alarming to know that, even by the developing standards of nations, one in every four people is living below the poverty line. On one side, we have a fast-progressing and so-called 'vibrant economy,' but on the other side, we have a population still struggling to come to terms with poverty. We cannot ignore poverty, which, in turn, is a factor for many other social problems like hunger, the spread of diseases, and an increase in crimes. To claim that the world is progressing and developing while around 1.4 billion people in the world are living in absolute poverty—below the poverty line —would be more than a farce.

Poverty is endured and created by people themselves, and it is the responsibility of people to eradicate it.

Poverty is a major cause of hunger-related deaths all around the world. According to the United Nations, about 25,000 people die every day from hunger, and many people do not have access to even a single meal. Poverty is also a cause of the spread of many contagious diseases, like pneumonia and tuberculosis. These disease are treatable, but in poor villages or communities, there are often no doctors or health centres for treatment. And if health centres or doctors are available, these poor people often unable to pay for or bear the cost of treatment and its requirements.

A child, who is born into poverty, undergoes extreme hardships during his growing up years. When they see children of his age having and enjoying all the luxuries of life, they may resort to short cuts to achieve those luxuries, which eventually leads to criminal behaviour. Thus, the rise in crime graph of a day can directly be attributed to the rise in poverty.

The UN definition of poverty is: "Fundamentally, poverty is a denial of choices and opportunities, a violation of human dignity. It means a lack of basic capacity to participate effectively in society. It means insecurity, powerlessness, and exclusion of individuals, households, and communities. It means susceptibility to violence, and it often implies living on marginal or fragile environments, without access to clean water or sanitation."

In today's modernized world where fast-food joints and malls have mushroomed in every nook and corner of the city, we can still see people outside these complexes begging for food and money. We still see mothers with their infants on their shoulders begging for money at traffic lights. We ignore them and move on, sometimes dismissing them as criminals who are part of the begging motion. In reality, do we care for them? Do we ever think about how their daily lives would be?

I myself belong to a farmer community. My ancestors were farmers. A small peasant brought up entire family through hard times by the dint of his hard work. This wits and vision made us and our family renowned in society. A vision of great soul, a great man Late Ch. Chandgiram. He inspired his sons to pursue education and gain knowledge. Slowly, his efforts converted a farmer family into officers with great identities. This was an example of a poor and simple peasant family became famous and cultivated linage.

My dear friends, what I want to elaborate on is that education is the only way to uplift yourself and stand at the top of world. Today in India, our farmers are getting education. They are doing well in fields as well as in others prospective. They are holding jobs and trying their luck in business. Outer incomes started flowing in and now he is capable in using new methods in his field to get more and maximum yields from it.

Farmers are the backbone of the nation. They provide food to the nation. They dig out the resources from the heart of land and distribute them. Even birds and animals meet their end on his tender attitude. He feeds them with grains, water, and even fruits. Some part of his output is consumed by birds and animals without any profit. Do we, or do you?

Not pointing anyone out, we know them every well. Jatas, Gujars, Patels, Ahir etc., have been predominantly agrarian communities in our society. One must not forget that, despite a section of people from these agrarian communities entering different occupations, disproportionately large numbers of them still depend on agriculture for their livelihood. The crisis in agriculture, which has witnessed returns becoming poorer and poorer in recent decades, has meant crises in their daily lives, leading them to face extreme hardships. While farming used to provide good returns, these people hardly faced financial crises and, hence, hardly bothered to seek government jobs.

But now, the time has changed. Due to poor rainfall and limited resources, farmers are heading toward peril. The decimation their yields due to climatic changes is driving them to suicide. Very few people are doing well due to fertility and water resources of their land, but the rest are facing troubles. They are falling and being placed at the lower rungs of society.

Only education can help uplift them and enable them to step ahead from the lower rung of ladder. Through education, youth can get absorbed in government and private jobs. They can support their family once they get salaries regular. They can also upgrade their farming skills and financial conditions. Initially, farmers had no financial resources, so they had to work with some very tight constraints. But now, due to vast and irrefutable facilities of education, a farmer can also reach his pinnacle. He can now break through an impermeable barrier by getting educated and absorbed in jobs or some other work.

Every time, and from time to time, rulers and governments always muzzle the voices of farmers.

Farmers and labourers are relegated every time and everywhere. They are always in fear —fear of failure, fear of dying hunger, fear of death, etc. The fear of failure is the most paralyzing of all human emotions. It stops us from trying, daring, and succeeding. It must be confronted.

Every great improvement has come after repeated failure. The greater the chance of failure, the more attractive and rewarding the success appears.

So, my dear farmers and poor workers, keep working hard and try to overcome all difficulties by educating yourself.

There is no time left to free yourself. One try is always a try. No one can fetter you or your dreams. There is a lot to do ahead, a lot to achieve ahead. Just try to step ahead.

Again, I sat alone for a while in silent contemplation, pondering over the plight of framers in our country. I often delve into pensive mood. Hardly any changes have been made in their lives and conditions since independence. Only a few have reached the summit, and rest are still trying.

Farmer is the frame of our nation. If the frame is strong, our image of a strong nation will be safe and sound; if not...? (page 28) Peril invigorates the farmer to upgrade himself and the nation. The existence of life of farmer on earth is irrefutable. The existence of intelligence and vibrant life is still hotly debated. But why only debated every time with no result?

From cornrow to twilight, a farmer has to struggle a lot with natural calamities. Sometimes drought, sometime heavy rainfall, always threatening his dreams. Such people of mercurial rainfall disturbs his crop schedule. In this way, he is been regularly beaten by nature since very beginning.

Apart from this, his pain does not vanish. His social and financial conditions continue to hinder his overall developments. "Starvation is not caused by lack of food but by lack of economic access to food."

So, our government must take positive steps to protect their farmers from being dying of hunger.

Every time, our politicians hope to launch a new scheme to attract the farmers, but planning for these schemes is still in its embryonic stage. They make false promises to attract farmers to fill their vote banks, rather than truly helping them. Every time they bal....(page 29) They, meaning a bevy of political leaders.

Our country is a land of farmers. Entire nation is united by the social fabric lunen (page 29) by our farmers. But simultaneously, this social fabric is being nibbled by the policies made by a few politicians, as well as industrialist. increasing in numbers of industries and other infrastructures decimating day by day.

There is a problem galore regarding forming. Shall we be able to solve the problems and overcomes the difficulties.

The future of agriculture depends on the efficiency of small landholdings. If we are to derive maximum benefit out of them, we have to solve the problems of small farmers. Our politicians and agriculture scientists must meet with farmers firsthand to acquaint themselves with their burning problems. For this intrinsic urge must be there in our leaders. Because of their intrinsic urge for farmers betterment and in depth study of their needs, suggestions like remedies for amelioration of their lot.

Mahatma Gandhi used to say, "Discover India in its villages. Our vast country is spread across small villages, and when we say of Indian village, a picture of a simple farmer comes in front of our eyes immediately."

A farmer in India is a basic unit of Indian economy. Farming or agriculture is his livelihood. A man strongly built, wearing a dhoti, kurta and a turban on his head can easily be marked as an Indian farmers.

He gets up early in the morning and gets ready for his daily routine. He goes to his field with his buns. He works in his field. His wife and sons assist him. He ploughs the field and sows seeds. He then waters them regularly. He is happy when he reaps rich yield and celebrates the occasion.

The calendar of his farming is dependent on the monsoon rain. He gets good crop when it rains sufficiently and on time. But occasionally, he has to face dry or wet famines, when he may lose his entire crop. Then it becomes difficult to meet both ends.

But this gloomy picture of helpless and weary Indian farmer is changing rapidly. How is it so? Let's see. The wave of development has touched him as well. The government has paid heed to his plight and undertaken many farmer-welfare schemes. It has provided good means of transport and communication. It is executing many educational and medical schemes. So, the poor and illiterate farmers are becoming literate. They are learning good habits of sanitation and vaccination.

Good seeds and fertilizers are available to him. He can get good fodder for his cattle. The banks have reached the village. So, loan facilities are also available so that farmers can use modern farming equipment instead of the traditional ones. He can raise a gobar gas plant. He can raise the latest and new irrigation systems for a sure water supply. The government of India is supporting and encouraging agriculture by broadcasting programs on radio and TV, enlightening the farmers. The recent GAT contract has opened the worldwide market for agricultural outputs and products to the farmers. The Indian farmers are also welcoming these new changes and developments in farming. They are taking benefits from them and changing their traditional ways of farming. An Indian farmer is becoming more thoughtful and experimental in his farming. He does not prefer to grow the same crops far years together. He now tries different crops. The new concept of 'natural farming' is a revolution and a boon for the farmer. Countries like Israel also are giving co-operation to Indian farmers.

Nowadays, due to vast deforestation, the Indian farmers have to face grave problems like scanty rains, erosion of soil, and a decrease in the underground water level, etc. The government is trying to find firm solutions for these problems. Thus, an Indian farmers can no longer be pictured as a poor, illiterate villager. The rapid development in agriculture has assured him a bright future and a good standard of living, so that we may say, the prosperous India can be discovered in its villages.

But, sorry to say, that most of the schemes are false promises of politicians, or immediate need is to be executed despite being kept silent in the pigeonholes forever.

India is an agricultural country. Seventy percent of the Indian population are farmers. They are the backbone of the nation. They produce food crops and oilseeds. They produce commercial crops. They produce some raw materials for our industries. Hence, they are lifeblood of our nation

Agriculture is a main and strongest strand of any business. Raw materials needed in every factories or company are provided by agriculture. Agriculture does not constrain itself to grains only. It consists of dairy farming, poultry, sheep farming, horticulture, and vegetation, etc. They are all different branches of agriculture. And you know who take care of all those streams of agriculture? He is, more than anyone else, a farmer.

An Indian farmer is the giver of food to the people, to all practical purposes. He sweats for the nation.

His Daily Life-

An Indian farmer is busy day and night. He works in the sun and rain. He ploughs the land. He sows the seeds. He keeps watering the crops at night. He guards the crops against stray cattle. He guards the harvest against the thieves. He reaps the crops and carries them home. Bullocks are the priceless and precious possession of the Indian farmer. He takes case of his bullocks as if they were his children. His wife and children help him in his work.

His Financial Condition-

The Indian farmer is poor. His poverty is well-known throughout the entire world. He can't get two full meals a day. He wears a piece of coarse cloth. He can't give an education to his children. He can't provide fine clothes to his children. He can't give ornaments to his wife. The farmer's wife has to manage with a few pieces of cloth. Ornaments are all part of their dreams. The farmer's wife also works at home and in field as well. She cleans the cowshed. She gathers cow-dung and pats it into pancakes. She dries them in the sun and piles them up because she will use them as fuel during the wet monsoon months. The Indian farmer is harassed by the village touts. He is harassed by the moneylenders and tax collectors. Hence, he can't enjoy his own yield.

The Indian farmer does not possess a suitable residence. He has no good house to live in. He lives in a straw-thatched mud cottage. His room is very small and dark. Only an oil lamp is used to light the cottage. Every time his cottage is ready to leak in the monsoon. The wedding of his children, especially daughters, depends on his yield. But my friends, let me tell you one thing: farmer's yield is always taken by village moneylenders or by landlords. Only a handful of his yield remains behind for his family to meet their ends.

Such plight! My hand is shivering writing all this. A farmer is always laden under the depth of lack. All his dreams and desires are trampled by the rich and powerful men. O' God! Please help him.

His Social Life-

The Indian farmer celebrates social function in the simplest manner possible. He celebrates many festivals throughout the year. He celebrates the wedding of his sons and daughters. But as I told you above, his children's marriages depend on his agricultural yield. He entertains his kith and kin, friends, and neighbours. He goes to visit his relatives; he attends open-air dramas and folk dances in his locality.

The condition of the Indian farmers should be improved. He should be taught the modern methods of farming. He should be made literate. So, many schools should be opened for them. He should be assisted by the government in all possible ways. Because upon his well-being, depends on the welfare of our nation and its people.

Point to be concerned in the book-

1. What kind of country is India?
2. Who is the basic unit of its economy?
3. Where does he live? Where does he wear?
4. What type of work does he do?
5. What kind of life does he live?
6. What are his means of livelihood?
7. What is his income?
8. Does he use modern technology?
9. What is the Indian government doing to improve his condition?
10. Has he made any development and progress?

Our farmers and scientists worked to overcome the challenge of self-sufficiency in food grain production with an impressive performance.

It's very clear that the benefits of the Green Revolution have not been shared in the same proportion by all sections of farmers. It has widely benefited the big farmers at the expense of small peasant farmers who lost their land to big farmers, tenants losing their security, and agriculture labourers receiving lower wages. The critics of new agricultural growth strategy felt that the growth in productivity has resulted in increasing poverty for large sections of India's rural population. In some cases, moreover, negative changes have added up to an absolute decline in the standard of living... payments for harvesting and even cash payments for day labour have remained stationary in the face of rising prices.

The rural folk got attracted to the imagery world of television and developed a desire to pursue those images and, in the process, thought of earning more and more. This further encouraged commercial agriculture, and the rural areas, which were known for simple living, warmth, strong values, and bonds of culture, underwent rapid changes. Today, the masses living in villages are neither ruralites nor urbanites and are struggling in a transition. Today, this change in the rural society affected farmers, especially young farmers, and as a consequence, the joint families, with their inherent advantages, broke into nuclear families, leading to fragmentation of land holdings and the requirement of separate infrastructure for each small family. Small fragmented land holdings, coupled with a horde of problems like erratic weather conditions, ignorance, and an imbalance in output-input ratio in farming, have affected their lifestyle.

Whether we like it or not, the fact of our rural life today is that our agrarian system is characterized by substantial inequalities in land ownership and use. A small fraction of India's rural population owns and operates more than half of India's arable land, while the rest are small landholders, tenants, and agricultural labourers.

The 'Green Revolution' has accelerated the process of turning this small class into affluent farmers. They produce for the market, using machinery, which results in reduction of the wages of agricultural labourers, pushes small farmers out of business as they cannot afford the costly inputs of modern agriculture, and displace village artisans as this new class purchases urban mass-produced consumer goods. The result of the expansion of this kind of agriculture is, thus, a widening of relative inequalities. This is due to the fact that agriculture has been ignored from the very beginning of our planning process, and farmers across the country are not getting their due.

The only difference is that farmers of Telengana and other arid zones are too poor. The farming community in other rural regions of the country is sometimes able to tolerate the shock of consecutive crop failures and are forced to commit suicides in order to save their honour, whereas they somehow are sustaining themselves. But their children are deprived of the fruits of development.

In order to trace the root cause of the problem in our agricultural sector, we have to go back to the phase when we attained independence and our planning process began. Agriculture is more important than anything else, not excluding big plants, because agriculture production sets the tone for all economic progress. If we fail in agriculture, then we fail in industry too. Agriculture is more important than industry for the simple reason that industry depends on agriculture. Industry, which is no doubt important, will not progress unless agriculture is sound, stable, and progressive. Jumping from a rural society to urban industry, no doubt, entails progress and development, but it has resulted in unemployment, poverty, disease, and destitution.

We should promote small farmer initiatives and provide policy packages stressing group endeavours during the next decade to remain self-sufficient in food production. However, small farmers face problems such as loans, cost of production inputs, risk factors, fragmented holdings, difficulties in efficient land and water management, saving money for reinvestments, and the like. The future of our agriculture depends on the efficiency of small farmer holdings, and if we have to drive maximum benefit out of it, we have to solve the problems of the small farmers.

Giving subsidies in a way that small and marginal farmers can derive economic benefits from new technologies. Saving water is not enough. There should be a common effort to promote the sharing of water and natural resources.

There are several factors for the decline in the growth rate, including the absence of land reforms, inadequate consumption of inputs like fertilizers and seeds, and inadequate irrigation. Irrigation is vital for agriculture, and agriculture forms the backbone of the country's economy. Due to able constraints of resources, there has been a shortfall in the financial provisions by the government to the farm sector.

Farmers are the ones who provide us all the food that we eat. As a result, the entire population of the country depends upon farmers. Farmers are the most important people in the world. Though farmers have to so much importance, still they do not have proper living conditions.

There are different types of farmers, and they all have equal significance. First are the farmers who grow crops like wheat, barley, rice, etc. Since the maximum intake in Indian households is of wheat and rice, the cultivation of wheat and rice is predominant in farming. Moreover, farmers who grow these crops are of prime importance. Second, are the ones who cultivate fruits. There are many other farmers who grow different types.

In addition, farmers contribute almost 17% or more of the Indian economy. That is the highest of all. But still, a farmer is deprived of the luxuries of society.

The condition of farmers in India is critical. We are hearing of suicides among farmers who have been living difficult lives for many years. The problem is they are not getting enough returns.

Since middlemen get most of the money, farmers gets nothing in hand. Moreover, farmers do not have money to send their kids to school. Sometimes the situation gets so bad that they don't even have proper food. As a result, they attempt suicides.

Furthermore, the other reason for the worst condition of farmers is global warming. Since global warming is affecting our planet in every way, it affects our farmers too. Because of global warming, there is delay in the seasons. As different crops have their own seasons to ripen, they are not getting proper nourishment. Crops need proper sunlight and rain to grow. So, if the crops are not getting either of these, they get destroyed. This is one of the main reasons why farms are getting destroyed. As a result, farmers commit suicide.

In order to save farmers, our government is not paying any heed. Our leaders make false statement with loud voices. They make such statements just to grab their votes. Our leaders make false promises in their speech to attract farmers so that they can win their elections. Once they win, they do not even look back to farmers. Farmers are once again lost in darkness, waiting for the day to shine ahead.

Farming is a profession which is full of toil and efforts. Moreover, seeing the growth of our population, we should take initiatives to help farmers of our country. Farmers are attempting suicides because their profession is not providing them even food to eat. Moreover, their farms are getting destroyed. As a result, it leaves them with nothing.

Farmers are the backbone of our country. All the economic development in the farming community is taken care of on a priority basis. The agriculture industry contributes more than 15%

of India's GDP. But unpredictable climate conditions, no proper pricing in place, and lack of help from the government are what is leading to farmer distress in the country. India has one of highest farmer suicide rates in the world. The Food corporation of India buys produce directly from farmers and stores it in their cold storage units for use during emergencies.

Farmers work hard every time. In any season, either winter, summer, or even during heavy rainfall, they work throughout. For them, there is no difference between days and nights. They keep on working hard every time. There is no period of rest in their lives.

All humans depend on agriculture for food. Urban industrial societies depend on the base of food surplus generated by farmers and herders. Without agriculture, there could be no villages, cities, universities, factories, or other offices. Today, agriculture remains the most important economic activity in the world. Agriculture employs 45% of the working population. In some parts of Asia and Africa, over 80% of the labor is engaged in agriculture.

On seeing such an importance of agriculture, we must fully support our farming community with a generous heart. We have to understand their requirements and needs. We must study their lives and livelihoods.

As we have mentioned earlier, farmers are the lifeline of the trajectory of the Indian agricultural setup. Farmers not only decide the crop yield of a season but also the types of crops being produced.

The world's first profession is farming. When man came into existence, he started hunting animals for his livelihood. He ate raw meat like beasts and wore wear skin of dead animals to protect himself from heat and cold. He used to live in caves to protect himself from other wild animals. Time passed, and gradually, he started doing farming. Necessity is the mother of all inventions. His desired and requirement for food led him to invent farming ways simultaneously.

Examples are there for farming doing by early man. Indus Valley civilization is the best example of it. Nomadic people gathered together and settled down on the banks of Sindhu river. There they got plenty of water for irrigation. They started farming in a well-planned manner. They used oxen for ploughing land and worked hard. They cultivated a large amount of land and improved their livelihood. Simultaneously, they formed two cities were the centre of development in those days. When these Aryans were in developed conditions, the entire Europe was still in the Stone Age. In the Indus Valley civilization, there was prosperous farming, education, business, and well-planned infrastructure.

So, in this way, we can say that our economy is based on agriculture since the very beginning. We must pay attention to farming and its requirements. We farmers need noble people to think positively about them, not people with atrocities. People who think of the Indus valley civilization, where progress and improved lives were achieved by doing farming, should ask, why can't we do the same now? Through farming, they started manufacturing pots, ploughs, and other farming equipment, etc. They started minting coins made of metal. The dancing girl sculpture is an example of their art. It means, with the help of agriculture, we can build and make anything. Base of every development is agriculture because raw material comes from here. Farmers in those days were happy and well-off. They met all their needs as well as give complete share to government for the development of their people and their culture. There was a proper work attitude in those old days. There was a complete nexus between farmers and businessman. They never interfered in each other's work. They helped each other in need. There was complete peace that entails development and progress. What I want to elucidate is, why can't we develops such environment for ourselves so that we can develop more and more? Once we join hands, our country will be the world power again, like in Gupta Dynasty. Again, we will be called a golden sparrow. A step, a day, is not far.

An Indian farmer should be respected by everyone. It is he who produces grains and vegetables for the citizens of the country. Throughout the year, the Indian farmer remains busy in tilling the fields, sowing seeds, and reaping the crops. Indeed, his life is very busy and hard.

A farmer works tirelessly to provide us with the food we need to survive. Despite the hard work, many farmers face challenges such as poor soil quality, lack of access to modern technology, and insufficient government support. These challenges have led to widespread poverty and distress among farmers. However, with the help of government initiatives and technology, the situation is gradually improving. Farmers are now able to access better seeds, irrigation, and financial support. This has led to an increase in crop yields and improved livelihoods for many. This is what we hear from Parliament or from our ministers daily. Does it seem true? Facts and something else.

Today, despite many developments, the situation of farming is deteriorating. Big farmers are becoming rich due to their side businesses and jobs. But most of the farmers are facing the same challenges every day. They are living in devastating conditions.

A line from a farmer-

Let the wrinkles dance across our faces,

Telling the story of our tears and laughter

Let our waistlines expand in tribute to

How much life we have tasted.

I myself have done farming. I can understand the plight of the farmers. They work hard every time, every day, and night. There is no proper schedule for the farmers. They work from very early morning till late at night. They plough the land under the scorching heat with no proper robes on them. They water the fields in winter nights too. They have to face many challenges like irregular rain, famine, heat storms, etc. His calculations never meet his requirements. Lot of input with little output. Sometimes leaving empty lands.

Farming is a noble profession. It is directly attached to the nature. A farmer creates nature by maintaining its purification by taking care of soil, water, air, animals, birds, insects, etc. He never harms anyone on the earth. He is the kind of father who nourishes every creature. Mother Earth and the farmer is like the father. Both feed everyone and provide every material and mineral to the world. So, do respect both Mother Earth and the farmer. Everything starts from scratch. Farming is the scratch, the base of everything.

Every profession starts from farming. Even our cultivated society is once part of the farming community. Gradually and simultaneously, people from farming switched to different occupation accordingly. Some became businessmen, some joined jobs, etc. But the reality is that their roots are still farming. So, pay full respect to the farming occupation and give equal status to farmers as you. Once farmers and businesses walk hand in hand, see how our country will rise like a sun. Again, we will be able to be known as a Golden Sparrow in the world.

Happiness, a highly subjective affair, defines a clear definition, but achieving it remains the ultimate aim of everyone. Since different people find happiness in different things, there is no universal formula for what makes people feel happy. But the universal truth remains that the role played by the state government can go a long way in making people feel satisfied and content. That satisfaction and contentment carry the ready-to-sprout seeds of happiness can hardly be overstated. If the government wants to see gaiety on the faces of people, it has to be practical, not in books or within the A.C. rooms. Laws should be made in favour of farmers and labourers but with full and complete execution. Provide full wages to labourers and a complete and profitable price for the farmers' yield. In this way, you will find happiness on the faces of all people.

Our country is known as a Krishi Pradhan Desh since very beginning. But does it sound well? Is it true? A country where a farmer is being tormented and compelled to commit suicides still boasts of being Krishi Pradhan Desh? Look at the crony of fate: a person who feeds the entire nation sleeps with an empty stomach. Their women and children, with half naked bodies, work on big and rich farmer's lands for wages. Their wives have to sleep with big money-lenders or big landlords for the debts they could not return. Their children have to work every day with little to eat throughout day and night, like bondage labour.

I could not think, a creator of food, a god-like image of a farmer has to face music every time throughout his life. Whatever he produces, he himself is deprived. Why? Why is it so? My heart starts melting whenever I ponder over this plight. My heart started sinking.

The farmer is a man who first ploughed mother Earth. He is a man who understood the nature of the earth and climate. He is, what I say, the first scientist on earth. He discovered and invented the methods of farming through work. He discovered plants in deep forests to produce fruits to eat. He is the first person who created fire by using stones and with further technological advancements. This illiterate man has given a lot to the world. Then how can we predict that he is illiterate? He is a practical man rather than theoretical one. Theories were written after his discoveries and inventions. He is the first person on earth who tamed animals and started making domesticating wild animals. Cows, buffaloes, horses, donkeys, sheep, goats, camels, and even elephants were among them. So, we can say he is a man with proper physique and brain. First, he started taking shelter in caves and then, slowly, slowly, simultaneously, started making huts and mud houses, etc. In this way, we can say he was the first architect on earth. He discovered and invented different and new methods to build huts and houses. So, please never underestimate the power of a farmer. A man who can grow seeds can build anything. There is a history that tells us about how a farmer switched to a soldier. A man from soil always serves soil in the name of a farmer as well as a protector like a soldier. So, we can't ignore these men who works for food as well as protect us from invaders. Our Late Prime Minister Sh. Lal Bahadur Shastri once said a slogan, *"Jai Jawan, Jai Kissan."*

In the present socio-economic structure, farmers are the backbone of society. Almost all the food items taken by us are produced by the farmers. Hence, whole population of the country depends upon the farmers. An economy can thrive because of the tireless work of the farmers. They are the most significant individuals on the planet. However, in spite of rigorous activities for our wellness, the farmers do not have proper living for themselves in most of the countries. Nearly 17% of the Indian economy is contributed by agro products that are produced by the farmers.

The situation of farmers in India has never been quite satisfactory for many years now. Poverty is their permanent companion. The major problem behind the condition of farmers is the middlemen. Farmers are not paid directly from the market because of the middlemen. The middlemen grab the lion's share of profit, leaving behind almost nothing for the farmers. They can't send their kids to schools or even feed themselves properly. As a result of this poor condition, they are compelled to end their lives.

Another major reason behind the plight of farmers is global warming. Since this is a global problem, farmers are the worst affected by it. Crops are getting damaged due to lack of proper nutrition. Seasons are getting delayed. As a result, reason-specific crops can't get proper sustenance. Many farmers are getting destroyed because of this.

The government has taken so-called steps to save the farmers. Various schemes have been implemented so far for the benefits of farmers. But all are gimmicks. Neither the benefits nor any schemes are useful to farmers. They remain buried in files. Due corruption, all schemes and benefits remain somewhere in between.

Farming is such a profession where extensive labour and effort are required. Farmers are the assets of our country. They should be treated like the soldiers of the nation. The steps taken by the government are not adequate to solve all the problems of the farmers. As responsible citizens of the country, we have to come forward to save the farmers of our country because we can't survive without them.

Farmers in India are in dire condition. Every month, we see news of farmer suicides. Furthermore, farmers have all had a rough existence in recent years. The issue is that they do not receive adequate compensation. A farmer receives nothing in hand since the intermediaries receive the majority of the money. Furthermore, farmers do not have the money to send their children to school. Sometimes the situation is so bad that they don't even have enough food to eat. As a result, farmers face hunger. As a result, they make attempts. Farmers commit suicide as a result of poor crops, low prices and loan.

One of the leading causes of global poverty is environmental deterioration, typically felt most acutely by smallholder farmers and indigenous people. Agroforestry with a social effect provides rural communities with food security and access to value chains for forest and food product. Common land began an enormous landscape restoration project in central India at the start of 2019. Simply put, the goal was to bring all parties and activities together into a single comprehensive restoration project with the capacity to expand.

A well-planned projects with a social benefit regenerates projects with a social benefit regenerates soil, maintains existing forests, improves water retention, and increases biodiversity in the environment. Greater yields result in more revenue, which allows these agricultural communities to fulfil their basic human requirement while also taking pleasure in the environment in which they live.

We have a lot of stories of farmers' fatalities which crush our hearts. Farmers commit suicide due to drought, the burden of loans, and agricultural losses. They encounter a variety of agricultural concerns and obstacles. Poorly maintained irrigation systems and a lack of adequate extension services are two of them. Poor roads, insufficient market infrastructure, and heavy regulation impede farmers' market access. Due to lack of investment, India lacks adequate infrastructure and services for farmers. Because most farmers have limited plots of land, they are forced to adopt conventional agricultural practices, sparing production. Farmers with larger plots of land, on the other hand, use contemporary agricultural practices, increasing outputs.

If small farmers wish to enhance their output, they must employ high-quality seeds, adequate irrigation systems, innovative agricultural instruments and procedures, herbicides, fertilizers, and so on. They require money for all of this; therefore, they have little alternative except to incur debt or obtain a loan from a bank. They are under enormous pressure to produce crops to prosper. If their crop fails, all of their efforts will be for naught. In fact, they are unable to create enough to even feed their families' bellies. They are unable to repay the debt in this scenario, and many of them commit suicide as a result.

Rural India is changing, but there is still a long way to go. Farmers have profited from new farming practices, although development has been uneven. The goal should be to prevent farmers from migrating to cities. To make agriculture viable and lucrative, adequate attention must be paid to improving the conditions of marginal and small farmers. Finally, farming is a career that requires a lot of hard work and effort. Furthermore, given our country's rising population, we should take proper steps to assist our farmers.

A bout of stormy weather brought heavy rain and hail, and more misery for the agriculture sector, with farmers fearing significant damage to key crops and held-up harvesting. Most states of the country have faced inclement weather, which began around mid-March, set off by back rain-bearing systems known as western disturbances and cyclonic patterns. The main concern with wheat is not so much about a fall in output but damage to quality of grains. Farmers done with harvesting are bringing soggy and discoloured grains to market, which affects their price. Is there any fault of farmers? They worked hard from scratch and ended with losses. Why? They did everything very well with proper planning of farming techniques. All their expenditure and household purchasing depends upon their sale of products like grains, vegetables, fruits, etc. But at last, due to inclement weather, farmers remain with empty hands. Either farmers have to change their farming patterns accordingly with climate change, or have to accept different agriculture with different farming methods. O' God, please pay heed towards your poor children who feed the entire world. Please help farmers, God, please.

Try to look back in our history. India suffered lots of problems at the time of pre-independence. Famine came—ghastly, staggering, horrible beyond words. In Malabar, in Bijapur, in Orissa, and above all, in the rich and fertile province of Bengal, men and women and little children died in their thousands daily for lack of food. They dropped down dead before the palaces of Calcutta; their corpses lay in the mud huts of Bengal's innumerable villages and covered the road and field of its rural areas. Men were dying all over the world and killing each other in battle — usually a quick death, often a brave death, death for a cause, death with a purpose, death which seemed, in this mad world of ours, an inexorable logic of events, a sudden end to the life we could not, would not or could not control. Death was common enough everywhere.

While the fires of hell were consuming the people of Bengal and elsewhere, no relief was there from the government. All false statements were declared that the peasanty in many parts of India had too much to eat. All were gimmicks.

Something was done at last. Some relief was given. But a million had died, or two millions, or three even. No one knows how many starved to death or died of disease during those months of horrors. No one knows of the many more millions of emaciated boys and girls and little children who just escaped death then but are stunted and broken in body and spirit. And still, the fear of widespread famine and disease hovers over their heads. Looking back, our farmers were dying like animals due to hunger.

The situation in modern time: farmers are still going through the same scenario. Every year, in Latur, Maharastra, farmers face drought and remain without food and money. A number of suicides occur across there. The government hardly pays attention towards them and their difficulties. Only at time elections, they visit to these farmers and but once elections over, these leaders never look back at the farmers again. Ministers fill the stomachs of farmers with their false statements or bombastic promises, which they never fulfill.

Many films were also made on the farmers and their plight. They reflect the miserable conditions of farmers and their lives. There was an epic, tragic, and poignant movie in 1957 named 'Mother India'. This movie reflects the irony of fate of a mother, who raises her children in very hard conditions. Radha, a poor but righteous woman, struggles to raise her children while going up against Sukhilala, a greedy moneylender. Despite the many hurdles she faces, she refuses to sacrifice her integrity. In this melodrama, a poverty-stricken woman raises her sons through many trials and tribulations. But no matter the struggles, she always sticks to her own moral code. Cinema's seminal epic about a grassroots-level Indian family whose fate forever hangs on the caprice of several obdurate forces. The grain of rice on your table does not tell the grim tale of the toil that grew it.

In this way, farmers suffer always. They do, they give, but never get. In the past three decades, India has made tremendous progress in food production due to Green Revolution. However, the benefits of Green Revolution with high-input modern technology have been predominantly confined to favourable farming situations. Only a few districts of India account for 25% of the national food basket. Thus, the lower productivity over a greater part of the country calls for an alternative pathway for ameliorating the situation to benefit a large number of small landholders in fragile and problematic environments.

The production system in drylands, covering around two-thirds of the cultivated area, is characterized by not only low productivity but also lesser stability, greater risk, and unemployment, which affect the economic condition of farmers.

Fulfillment of this gigantic task will not be an easy proposition, as it has to cover a large number of resource-poor farmers operating fragmented small holdings in harsh environment.

Thus, in the farming system approach, major emphasis is given to developing board-based package of technology for optimization of resources on a farm to attain higher agricultural returns on a sustainable basis without impairing the quality of the environment.

In India, akin to other developing countries, majority of farmers belong to the category of marginal to small landholders. As their resource-use capabilities are low, their farming activities remain, by and large, subsistence in nature rather than commercial.

Self-reliance for household food needs has been an issue of primary importance to many millions of them. However, the farmer is not working in isolation. His farming activities are constantly influenced by biophysical, social, and economic factors.

We had an eminent personality who lived and died for the upliftment of farmers in India. Sir Chhota Ram was a prominent politician in British India's Punjab province, an ideologue of pre-independent India who belonged to the Jat community and championed the Jat community and especially farmers, and championed the interest of oppressed communities of the Indian subcontinent.

Sir Chhota Ram was born on November 24, 1881. He graduated from St. Stepen's College, Delhi, in 1905 with a distinction in Sanskrit. He did his L.L.B. from Agra college in 1910 and began his practice as an advocate in 1912. He was then the revenue commissioner of Punjab province. He was popular among Muslims too. Pathans used to call him Chootu Khan. He was regarded as a messiah of peasants and was instrumental in empowering farmers in pre-independence era. He also played a significant role in enacting pro-farmers laws. He is a revered figure in Haryana's Jat community and is also known as a champion of farmers' rights during the British colonial era. Sir Chhotu Ram was knighted in 1937.

Sir Chhotu Ram contributed a lot to farmers and the development of the country. He conceived of the Bhakhra Dam, in 1923, to relieve the farmers of the economic plague-spots of erstwhile Punjab state.

He was also the originator of the concept of compensating the farmer for at least the expenses incurred by him on farming. He exhorted peasants to shed their inferiority complex and fatalistic outlook and become assertive and self-confident. He encouraged agriculture-based industries as well as the development of cottage industries in the state to tackle the problem of unemployment in both rural and urban areas. He rightly recognized the problems of agriculture, such as unfair taxation, high rates of land revenue, inability to secure fair prices for their production, the crushing burden of indebtedness, and expenses on litigation.

He also noted that illiteracy and ignorance, underrepresentation of the class of peasantry in the public services, corruption, and the frequent occurrence of farmer protest added to the woes of the farmers.

He used to recite the following lines of the poet Iqbal quite often:

"Raise thyself to such
A height that God
May himself ask you
What do you wish to achieve."

खुदी को कर बुलंद इतना
कि हर तकदीर से पहले
खुदा बंदे से पूछे
बता तेरी रज़ा क्या है

He ameliorated the condition of the farmer community. He accumulated the farmers and made them stand on their feet. A huge unity of farmers, as well as common people, was with him. Till today, Sir Chhotu Ram is like God to farmers, especially Jats. Today, such hard time is going on specially farmers, that they are facing critical situations and conditions. Their land is being acquired by the Government as well as big businessman in name of development. Everywhere, land is acquired in name of development and infrastructure. Especially fertile land is being forfeited or purchased for marginal profit. What will happen once all agricultural land is sold or acquired? Farmers will be left with nothing to do. In this way, gradually or rapidly, agriculture will vanish, and people will die of hunger. Because without grains, fruits, vegetables, etc., can it be possible to fill the bellies of people with merely money or other facilities?

I don't say that development is not needed. It is also a big requirement; infrastructure is most important in the development of our country. But agriculture is the base of everything. All raw materials and goods are produced by farming. Many kinds of medicines are made from plants and their ingredients. Textile industries are totally dependent on agriculture. Cotton, silk, wood, etc., are produced by farmers, as are shepherds and other farmers who farm cocoons for silk. Wood from sheep as well as goats. Milk is the most important ingredient in our lives. It is used by everyone on Earth. So many things are made from milk. And butter, cheese, etc., are so many products are made from milk. Now the question arises: from where does milk come? Do big businessmen produce milk, wheat, rice, barley, vegetables, etc.? All these things are produced by different farmers in different ways. If I am not wrong, 70% of materials comes from farming and its sister industries. We can't avoid it. Avoiding farming and its requirements would be our blunder. On chopping of our legs, can we stand or walk. Same is like if we try to ignore farmer and his problems, we'll be unable to live long.

Like Sir Chhotu Ram, another eminent personality from farmer community, Chaudhary Charan Singh served the farmers community with great enthusiasm. Chaudhary Charan Singh served as the 5th Prime Minister of India between 28 July 1979 and 14 January, 1980. Historians and people alike frequently refer to him as the champion of India's peasants.

In his cameo as Prime Minister, two-time Chief Minister of Uttar Pradesh, and Union home and Finance Minister, Chaudhary Charan Singh became the face of farmers and their needs. In his tenure, he introduced various policies to improve the lives and conditions of the farmers. The principal architect of the U.P. Zamindari Abolition Act, Singh also authored books on Zamindari Abolition, land reforms, and the establishment of an economically self-sufficient peasantry in U.P. To relieve the farmers of moneylenders, he introduced the Debt Redemption Bill in 1939 in the state assembly. The Land Utilisation Bill, drafted by Singh in April 1939, aimed to 'Transfer the propriety interest in agricultural holdings of U.P. to such tenants or actual tillers of the soil who chose to deposit an amount equivalent to ten times the annual rent in the government treasury to the account of the landlord."

Rooting for rural democracy, Singh opposed a resolution of joint, cooperative farming passed in 1959 by Congress, a party he defected from only to form the largest and most successful agrarian party in modern Indian polities.

Owing to the leader's contribution to India's agrarian concerns, Singh's memorial in New Delhi is named Kisan Ghat. Unwavering when it came to safeguarding the rights of hardworking farmers, Charan Singh Ji also worked tirelessly for the empowerment of the marginalized. He was at the forefront of strengthening India's democratic fabric."

Another farmer leader emerged with great heart for farmers: Chaudhary Devi Lal, an Indian statesman and politician who served as the 6th Deputy Prime Minister of India from 1989 to 1990 and again from 1990 to 1991.

He was born into a Jat Hindu family on 25 September 1914 in Teja Khera Village of Sirsa District in Haryana. Ch. Davi Lal, whose original name was Devi Dayal, received education up to middle school and also trained as a wrestler at an 'Akhara' in Badal village (Punjab).

After independence, Ch. Devi Lal started a farmers' movement and was arrested along with 500 workers. He also emerged as the leader of the farmers from Haryana. He became Haryana's Chief Minister, and soon his government passed an order that waived the outstanding loans of small farmers, agricultural labourers, and small businessman.

He was popularly known as "Tau" among people. Everyone used to call him Tau Devi lal. He was such a personality that just one word from Tau, a huge amalgamation of farmers started following him. No accurate numbers of people are there. Minimum lakhs of people were found where Tau ji stand. He did a lot for farmers. Farmers got full support from him and were invigorated under his tutelage.

Till today, like Sir Chhotu Ram Ji, Chaudhary Devi Lal ji remain in the hearts of farmers and common people.

The majority of the farming community was illiterate, but they were wise enough. They relied on the wisdom of their prior generations, which was beneficial to the community and no harm to the environment. They supplied only organic produce. Agriculture was never a commercial business. It was just a way of the life on which all other professions relied and wore interwoven. Unfortunately, the so-called bureaucrats and blind politicians simply copied Western policies, encouraging intensive cultivation of just 4 crops: rice, wheat, cotton, and sugarcane.

Rice and sugarcane are highly water-demanding, yet they were permitted even in water-scarce areas. Black and alluvial soils are suitable for cotton, but it is grown even in red soils.

We used to cultivate mavadhanyalu meaning nine types of cereals, millet, and grains. Now they are no more. Never concentrated on logistics and supply chains, there is still no value of addition to the produce.

Farmers were never taught how to use pesticides and fertilizers. Farming is in the clutches of middlemen, traders who supply substandard pesticides, fertilizers, and seeds, moneylenders, and politicians who frame policies for votes.

The farmer is aware of all this, but he is helpless. But, there is a silver lining on the positive side: a few young and energetic farmers are making a difference by educating their fellow farmers.

Today, in the month of March, a time for starting the harvest of wheat, it is raining simultaneously until 31st of March 2023.

Unwanted rain, and thunderstorms, and even hail have devastated the entire crops of farmers. All their desires vanished, and they were trapped in this devastating condition. The entire wheat crop is submerged in water and destroyed badly. Farmers can't harvest their crop, and even the seeds are in bad condition and small in size.

Masseet will create problem for farmers to purchase the crops. I don't understand what God wants from farmers. Have pity on them, God. Please! Already, there are many hurdles on the path of farmers, and now u even helping them, living them in devastated conditions. Living the farmers in peril. Every time they live in the condition of fear and harm. What are their fault? They worked hard with honesty and live innocently simple life. They never demand much accept the fruitfull result of their hard work. Farmers are very innocent and simple. They never demand any luxurious life. They just want peaceful life with their agricultural outputs. They just want the proper returns of their expenses. A community, who feeds energy, remains hunger. Their children sleep with very little loaf of bread or ever nothing. They live in huts and wear less roabs. Farmers are being always tormented by nature as well as system made by government and middlemen. Is any one their, who can listen their voices or problems. We all must help them. We must understand the scenario the farmer go through. Make some way out to uplift the farmers. One, the farmers get progressed, entire nation will automatically will develop and one day will be the richest country in the world. Nexus of culture, work and finance among everyone specially with farmers will entail progress and development in country. All will remain happy and prosperous. Please ponder about it. We can have positive results with fine colours.

It is ironical, but true, that after the introduction of the liberalization process, India is gradually being divided into two complexes: one is urban metro complexes, and the other is rural India. Wittingly or otherwise, the policy initiatives since the beginning of the 1990s, have concentrated on the needs of hi-tech communication and technological needs of the urban complexes.

High-speed techniques, seminars, and conferences on globalization, management, and people advocating virtues of competition and the free economy, total quality management, and so on, have invariably been concentrated in five-star hotels in the metros. The large rural masses, who produce grain, have remained untouched by liberalization. The new millennium and the associated type do not matter much to them.

Despite being the largest producer of milk and tea, the second largest producer of wheat, fruits, vegetables, sugar, and cashew, and the third largest producer of tobacco and rice, with the largest cattle population in the world, India's share in the world market for these products was not even one percent. A higher share was possible only through the joint efforts of the government and the trade. In recent years, agricultural trade has been totally liberalized. Minimum export prices have been announced, and most items have been decontrolled. Export infrastructure was proposed to be the focus of the Ninth Plan period, and efforts were made to address other problems, such as credit and trade barriers.

All the above plans are good here, but do they implement properly? Again, trade is given more importance, which benefits only big businessmen and middlemen. Farmers must have full rights to sell their products in markets according to their comfort.

They are the people who feed the whole nation. Let us take a small example to understand the importance of farmers in a better way. When we are hungry, we cannot stay without food. That food reaches our plates only because of farmers. Farmers make a huge contribution to the economy of any country.

The life of farmers is very simple and rooted to the ground. They and their family members who work on the farm wake up early in the morning and spend the whole day in the fields. They plough land, sow the seeds, water the crops, plant, and do their best to protect the field and yield. They then wait patiently for the harvest time. A farmer's life is simple. They don't look forward to many luxuries. They look forward to a good harvest and getting a reasonable price for their crops.

A farmer's social life is very different from city talk. They spend all day on the farms. From early morning until sunset, they toil in the fields. The farming activity requires such hard work that they get exhausted when they return home. Their social life is more or less meeting other farmers or people from their neighborhood post sundown and sharing their thoughts and problems.

The government must pay heed to the difficulties and problems of the farmers seriously. Leaders and bureaucrats bypass their problems. They never give importance to the farmers.

Unseasonal rain wreaked havoc on farmers. All their toil and patience were flooded with rainwater. All their crops are submerged beneath the water in the fields. Farmers are searching for the remaining bits of grains from the fields. All their desires and needs shatter. They are perturbed and confused, not knowing what to do. Grains in warehouses and mandis are also in bed condition. Proper facilities are not there to protect grains from such harsh weather to save the grains kept with them in the market. Such a critical condition of grain and farmers exists, but no proper solution is being initiated by the government. No one is taking it as a serious matter.

The government is forgetting the values of grains, especially in our country, where wheat is a major crop. Not only farmers are dying, but the impact will also be felt by the common man. The entire market will rise with growing prices, and how can the government declare that the cost will not rise in the market? Middlemen and businessmen will start playing games by holding onto market. They will decide to purchase the grains at very low prices according to their comfort and profit. They will mint money by selling the same grains at high prices to the common man and even to the farmers, who they bought the grains from at a profit for themselves. Farmers got nothing from the crop that they grew, whereas middlemen as well as businessmen became richer by selling the same crop on higher rates.

After excessive and unwanted rain and thunderstorms harmed the crops, farmers now face the daunting task of gathering their harvest and taking the produce to market without any labourers to help them.

Farmers in North India are staring at rain. Just as it was ripping, the winter crop was seriously damaged by untimely rainfall in March and April. Wheat, potato, chickpea, mustard, rapeseed, and vegetables were among the crops damaged in hail and thunderstorms in India.

March 2023 has been one of the rainiest on record in India. The beginning of April has been the same, with rain still falling and hailstorms occurring in some places. The excess rainfall in North India hides even grimmer numbers for some areas. Excess rain between March and April, seriously damaged the wheat crop that are ready to harvest.

Erratic rainfall due to a changing climate has added to India's farm distress in recent months. Changing rainfall patterns not only lead to extreme weather events, such as floods and droughts, but unseasonal rain or dry spells also harm food production.

Farmgate prices have crashed in many places due to supply bottlenecks. The farmer is caught between climate havoc and dead markets. He is moving to and fro in search of his satisfaction, but there seems no way for him to resolve his problems. He is jostling for satisfactory results with peace and gaiety.

Farmers all over India are plagued by several issues. These problems indirectly or directly affect farmers' life. Furthermore, farming practices and other aspects of agriculture can take up resources and time. The problems faced by farmers are typically unnoticed in food industry.

Farmers in developing countries have a hard time transporting their produce to markets due to lack of roads, vehicles, and money. They often have to carry their produce from the farm to the local market on foot, by bicycle, or bullock carts, which can be challenging and time-consuming. This means that they often have to sell their produce at very low prices because they cannot transport it to places where there is better demand for food.

Farmers need capital to get their business off the ground and grow it into successful operations. However, they often have little access to credit or financing because lenders don't understand their unique needs. The lack of financial resources affects not only productivity but also the quality of agricultural produce. Farmers in some villages do not have access to adequate funds to invest in better technologies, machinery, and equipment, which results in poor-quality agricultural produce.

Agricultural marketing refers to the process of bringing a product from the farmer to the consumer. It includes activities such as finding buyers for the products, negotiating prices, transporting goods, and getting feedback on quality. Because there are many people involved in this process, it can be quite challenging. Farmers have to find buyers who will pay them a fair price for their goods while also ensuring that they don't sell too cheaply or too expensively.

In many cases, they are forced to sell their products at a low price or even give them away because they cannot find buyers. This situation creates an incentive for small farmers not to produce more than what they need for their own consumption.

Irrigation is known to help improve agricultural production, and while irrigation methods have improved to help increase the income of farmers, there are still numerous irrigation-related hurdles that make it harder for farmers to get income commensurate with their expenditure.

Whether it's because of droughts, floods, or just low rainfall, irrigation can be difficult to maintain. Farmers have often been forced to fall back on groundwater resources when surface water sources dry up during droughts. In other cases, they've had no choice but to rely on groundwater even when adequate surface water is available. This can cause problems as underground water levels drop and farmers are unable to pump enough water to keep their crops alive through the dry season.

The quality of seed used in farming is essential in attaining a higher crop yield. It is also important in getting sustained growth in agricultural production. Distribution of high-quality seed is as important as seed production. High-quality seeds are typically out of reach for most farmers, especially marginal and small farmers, due to their prohibitively high prices.

One of the biggest issues that farmers face is lack of infrastructure. This includes poor roads, transportation facilities, and so on. Farmers have to depend on others for transport services, which increase their costs significantly. Without proper transportation facilities, it becomes difficult for farmers to sell their produce at reasonable prices within their respective locations or localities or even outside their villages or townships.

Farmers are unable to get good quality seeds, fertilizers, and even pesticides at reasonable prices. They also have to spend money on other inputs like irrigation systems, etc., which is quite high compared to other countries like China or U.S.A., where they have all the facilities available at their doorstep.

One of the major farmers' problems has to be loss of agricultural land, as when more land is lost, it becomes increasingly difficult to produce the right volume of crops required to feed the entire population. Lots of encroachment by private builders, big businessmen, and even the government are creating problems for farmers. Agricultural land is being rapidly captured by these people in the name of developing infrastructure. They started taking farming land from farmers at low prices and selling the same land to big businessmen for their benefits. If the companies or factories are established, the agricultural land will start decreasing day by day. The day is not very far when we will not find any food to eat because agricultural land is rapidly going out of farmers' hands, which entails scarcity of food. Development and infrastructure are needed for the nation, but not at the expense of farming. This is one of the major reasons why Indian farmers are not competent. Because most of the poor farmers have a very small amount of land, and that too in a fragmented manner.

The main reason for this kind of system is the inheritance law of India. When a person dies, the land belonging to him is distributed among his sons, but distribution does not ensure entailment of consolidated land. As a result, most of the farmers in India have fragmented lands.

In the absence of marketplace, local traders dominate the market, and the exploitation of farmers takes place. These middlemen are not only creating a problem for farmers but also consumers because they ultimately sell the crops at a very high price after purchasing them from farmers.

The situation of poor farmers is even worse. They are forced to sell their crops at whatever price is offered to them.

Going through these entire problems, how can we expect our farmers to produce good crops? Instead, we should ask our government to provide the facilities that they deserve.

Lack of access to credit is one of the most pressing issues that hinder India's rural population from progress. It means the lack of access to credit for a farmer. Farmers' suicide within the agricultural sector does not occur as a shocking matter as the farmers are deprived of monetary assistance when they are most in need. The lack of access to formal credit thus places many constraints on agricultural output and also on the standards of living for the rural population, thereby hindering their path to further economic and social development.

Overdependence on unreliable rain and lack of irrigation facilities has led to a decline in agricultural output. Poverty and illiteracy of the farmers prevent them from making large-scale capital investments and adopting scientific methods of cultivation and modern advanced farming. Small landholdings due to fast-growing population lead to fragmentation of land at quick succession. As a result, the size of the plot becomes smaller with every passing generation. This greatly hinders the process of farming. Erosion of soil by heavy rain, floods, insufficient vegetation cover, etc., reduces farm productivity. Inadequate irrigation facilities and poor management of water resources have led to a great deficit in agricultural productivity.

In this way, our farmers face lots of difficulties and problems. Every step they take, the have to halt and are unable to steadfastly move forward. Wrinkles on their faces tell the story of their miserable condition. Their rough and strong hands tell us about their hard work in the fields. Their bellies tell us who and how hungry they are.

Farmers face lots of hurdles. From ploughing to harvesting, and furthermore, marketing, they fall prey to exploitation by everyone. No one is there for their help. Even God bypasses their problems, even though farmers are the ones who pray to God with sincerity. They give respect to every person by saying, "Ram Ram ji". Even animals and birds are cared for; farmers feed cattle and birds without any wish except for peace. They are very simple people and live a simple life. They don't have any bombastic desires. They just only want the reasonable cost of their products. No hand comes forward to help farmers. O' God, they are the sons of the soil. Please help them. Please help your poor children. They are in need of you.

Their life is getting more and more difficult day by day. The condition of the farmers is getting from bad to worst. If something is not done urgently, there will be nothing left to save.

One of the major problems is flood. The havoc caused by floods many times has been equally devastating. Why did not the grant schemes succeed? Every time a flood occurs, politicians have a ready alibi: Deforestation in the hills and excessive rain, but the real blame lies with ad hoc government policies, which have perpetuated myopic flood-control measures, unchanged since the British days.

Dams were built, but adding to the problem is the fact that the money earmarked for repairs often ends up elsewhere. Most of the money allocated for repairs is pocketed by corrupt politicians, contractors, engineers, etc. The nexus of politicians, contractors, and engineers are the real culprits in any devastating situation. We must eradicate such corruption from our country fast; only then can fair work be done.

As a government boasts by saying that the basic needs for all citizens, especially farmers, have been completed and reached every nook and corner of the country, it is all gimmickry. There are many villages in India where such basic needs have not reached. Such villagers are in areas where there are no proper roads, electricity, hospitals, schools, etc. The villagers and farmers are still deprived of all basic infrastructure. And we are boasting about being like America or other European countries. A long path is ahead of us to compete with European countries and especially America.

Still, there lives too India. One urban and second is rural urban life is running fast whereas rural life is still crowing. The rich are becoming richer, whereas the poor are becoming poorer. There is a world of difference in both. We must create a proper nexus between urban and rural development equally. Then we can uplift ourselves and start in the pathq2222 of development.

We must curb our population immediately. The more the population, the more the requirements. One day will come when we will be unable to meet these requirements and needs. It will create havoc. Land is being fragmented day by day, and population is increasing rapidly. The farming area is reducing to a pulp, and will it be possible to grow more grain for a huge population from these fragmented farms? This is an alarming situation. The government, as we as we all, have to ponder over the entire devastating scenario.

Due to the increasing population, every resource will not be able to fulfill the demand, because resources are limited or even decreasing and vanishing. Proper planning is needed and must be executed honestly. We must follow the formula of live and let live. Help each other, whether rich or poor, urban or rural.

Even animals are suffering due to hunger. The increasing number of animals, especially in urban areas, is becoming a havoc. Stray cattle are found in large herds on roads and in cities. Why? What is the reason behind it? We, human, are to blame. We unleash the cattle after making them graze themselves. People in cities have not been able to keep cattle in good conditions. They take loans from banks in the name of cow sheds (Gau Shala). They keep cattle there for just a while and then set them free forever, once the sanctioned money is received by the banks. We must stop this poor practice.

Veterinary departments must keep a check on stray cattle. Castrate the stray cattle, so that they can't breed further. It is becoming tough to produce much fodder for the large number of cattle. Minimize the population of cattle and focus on good breeding and care. Create proper shelters and provide timely care and treatment.

Cattles like cows, buffalos, goat, sheep, pigs, and camels are part of farming. Even poultry farming is in abundance. They all are part of farming; without milk, eggs, meat, and other things, farming cannot succeed. We say they are domestic animals, so treat them like your family members. Take complete care of animals and don't unleash them to go scot-free. Graze them in your fields or at your houses where they are under shelter with proper fodder and care. Animal husbandry and poultry farms are also helping hands for farmers. They are no longer just cattle; they are also a business. Take care of the cattle, and they will help you in minting money. Proper planning must be done.

As mentioned before, usually there are two parts of the country. One is urban areas and the other is rural areas, and various numbers of livelihood opportunities are available there tin these areas as per the requirements or availability.

India's rapid economic expansion has attempted to include the rural population, which is concentrated in areas where rain-fed agriculture is the primary source of income. Poverty remains, however, due to restricted and inequitable access to productive resources such as land, water, improved inputs and technologies, and microfinance, as well as drought and other natural calamities. Low literacy and skills also conspire to keep people in poverty, preventing them from claiming their basic rights or engaging in additional activities that would earn them money or help them create assets.

It's not just about poverty alleviation. It's most important for people to stand on their feet and develop on their own. Often, people in rural communities have the knowledge, but there are not enough opportunities for them to apply it.

Whenever we think of rural India, what picture comes to our minds? A village, farmers, crops, livestock, etc. There are various farms and non-farm activities that are present which people use in rural areas to live their lives.

There are people who do not own agricultural land, and they used to work on other farmers' lands during specific seasons. They do not own permanent jobs, but only seasonal ones, like during sowing or harvesting season. The remaining days of the year, they are unemployed, which leads to seasonal unemployment.

There are rich farmers as well in the villages who own larger pieces of land and hire many other people to work, or sometimes even own mills or industries. These rich farmers lend money to others and exploit the weaker sections of society by charging large sums of interest.

Some challenges affecting rural livelihood include natural disasters and disease outbreaks. These pose serious threats to their livelihoods, with the poor being most affected. Some natural disasters include floods, earthquakes, storms, fires, and landslides. These natural disasters cause loss of life, property, and livelihood. Among the rural population, whose livelihoods depend on land and other natural resources, natural disaster deprive these communities of human capital. People lose crops, livestock, and sources of income, which leads to the loss of financial capital. Additionally, people lose their homes. The community is left trying to recover from the disaster. Because of the loss of income and income-generating resources, natural disasters can lead to poverty. The emergence of diseases after natural disasters further complicates the situation. Apart from these problems, the roads, electricity, telecommunications, and transportation facilities are in poor condition. Such a tough life do rural people and farmers face. The irony of fate.

Agriculture has remained a traditional forte of developing economies for a long time. Besides providing employment to a vast majority of the population in the developing world, it has provided food and raw materials for both urban and rural sectors and sustained, to a large extent, the export growth in these nations, especially India.

In order to offset the rising cost of cultivation and agricultural production based on high-priced imported inputs, developing countries like India will have to think of an expanded effort to generate low-cost appropriate technologies, inputs, and infrastructure, so that their comparative advantage in the agricultural and primary-producing sectors is perceptibly sustained.

However despite the great importance of the agricultural sector in the Indian economy, until recently, the extent of agricultural research has remained disappointingly low. Not only has agricultural research expenditure remained at its lowest level, but these has also been an abysmal lack of specialist research personnel in this area.

The current state of research in the agricultural sector in India is absolutely dismal. This does not augur well for the competitive strength of the Indian economy in the emerging milieu of globalization. If India's national priorities target providing cheaper and abundant food to our burgeoning population and aim at strengthening our competitive position in the international market, we must consolidate our conventional specialization in agriculture and primary-producing sectors by scaffolding them with strong R & D (Research & Development) programs.

Poverty is a disease, and economic liberation is a cure.

The measure is directed towards giving a boost to the economy, which lies in the doldrums even after half a century of achieving independence, and to divert from the hackneyed socialist approach, which has failed to meet its prime objective of eradicating poverty. Poverty lies in every nook and corner of our society.

The common man of India is not the one who pockets regular income and enjoys his life in cities, but instead is the one who depends exclusively upon agriculture and commerce to satisfy his basic needs. This is the bitter truth that the successive governments at the centre have failed to realise. Our economy is mainly agrarian, with nearly 70% of the population engaged in agricultural and related pursuits, and it is this community that constitutes the bulk of the poor.

Our farmers do not enjoy the kind of subsidy rates like their foreign counterparts, and thus the indigenous units prove incompetent against cheaper foreign goods, manifesting into large-scale unemployment and stunted growth in export. Thus, the reforms are in danger of boomeranging on us and disabling the economy permanently.

National investments in rural infrastructure and development have gone down largely because of debt service burden, the enormous cost of bureaucracy, pay commission commitments, and so on. There is hardly any money left for development. Such a plight do our farmers have to face. Proper channelization of resources is necessary to remove poverty.

In our country, as we open our economy to more sectors, especially agriculture, millions are in danger of being unemployed, adding to the endemic poverty. The false promises of providing a level playing field for India in eradicating poverty and in launching different schemes of employment and agricultural reforms do not address the conditions of farmers.

In many places in India, farmers still live in pitiable conditions, just as their forefathers did during the exploitative British Raj. The only difference now is the complexion and lineage of the exploiters. Economic liberalization and political independence are hollow jargon to the starving and blighted populace, especially in places where poor farmers die due to hunger. Even doctors refuse to serve in remote rural areas where they cannot make a fast buck.

Farmers' kids toil at the firework and carpet-weaving factories. Even in some areas in our mother nation, a pitiable and miserable mother has to sell her newborn baby for only a few coins to meet her end. A wife of a poor farmer goes through such a trauma. For these farmers, life continues to be a bed of thorns. Poverty continues to be the giant killer, and few can afford to give the medical care to their wounds given by poverty, a veil of death for them. The rich try to ram through the throats of countless poor farmers by exploiting them. Such incidents highlight the great social and economic disparities that the nation carries with it.

Fields such as education and health services, infrastructure, public sector management have been ignored, and thus, the farmer is denied his share of the benefits that liberalization brings with it. So, please pay heed to the poor farmers and provide them all their rights and benefits in these fields.

Pay heed to their muffled cries and wails of countless poor farmers on our motherland, as well as far away, and wipe their tears with the hands of support and care. Chalk out an effective plan to eradicate poverty among farmers.

In the name of consumerism, we have forgotten the Gandhian principles of non-violence and self-reliance. As a result, indigenous crafts are becoming extinct. It is all right to race ahead and join the others, but we must not forget the basic values of non-violence, simplicity, tolerance, and peace. Village industry should exist along with big corporations.

As such, we think that there is nothing we can do about poverty. Lack of political will to tackle it is the main cause of poverty in our country. Here, imparting practical education might be the right step. Poverty has to be tackled with sound economic programs. What we need is a management commission, not a planning commission.

We have failed to exploit natural resources and human skills. There is a lot of wastage of scarce resources like water. A lot of skilled labour is migrating to other cities or even other countries, though we have invested in their education. India is a vast country with abundant natural and human resources. We must exploit these resources, but not in a mindless way by destroying forests and the countryside. What we need is a sustainable development model.

The rich are becoming richer, and the poor are becoming poorer because of our economic policies. The poor have not benefited from the economic programs. Although we cannot do without massive industrialization and the private sector, we should make sure that the poor are not exploited by the rich and that the poor get a chance to live with dignity. But when and how? Our development programs should take into account the problems of the poor and the backward sections.

Frequent amendments will not make any difference. The problem lies with the way we work and perform, not with the constitution. The problem lies with us, not with the constitution. Proper and honest execution of laws and rights could make some difference.

States must be allowed to manage their own programs. Even at the village level, people should be involved in policy-making because a civil servant sitting in Delhi may not be aware of the ground realities. If local people are not consulted, it leads to unhappiness and unrest among them.

Jharkhand, India's one of the poorest and most food-insecure states, has over 45 percent of the population living below the poverty line. More than 75 percent of Jharkhand's citizens rely on farming for their livelihood, but agriculture accounts for only 15 percent of gross state domestic product. Groundwater depletion and periodic drought compound the state's difficulties and low agricultural productivity, even as a changing climate threatens to make the situation worse.

India's agriculture sector is projected to see a significant reduction in supply, demand, and value. Here's how we can safeguard farmers through it.

Additional support is needed to bolster the livelihoods of agricultural workers or farmers, who make up 58 percent of India's population. We anticipate farming households producing high-value cash crops, such as fruits and vegetables, to require the greatest support, as these crops tend to be perishable and, therefore, more vulnerable to supply chain disruptions and reduced demand.

Supply chain disruptions, including reduced transportation and storage capacity, stressed farmers' economics due to reduced household income and a potential increase in the cost of inputs, will impact production capacity in upcoming season.

Huge rain in March and April 2023 brought another set of worries for farmers. This is the problem of plenty, which seems to have driven down the prices of most agricultural commodities. As a result, farmers are running into losses because output has decreased.

Clearly, it is not the glut in agricultural markets which has resulted in the decline in prices of most agricultural commodities. The real reason lies in the distress in rural economy, which has led to a decline in the real incomes of rural populations. Despite claims of green shoots of economic recovery being projected by the mainstream media, the reality is that the rural economy continues to worsen.

While farmers continue to suffer due to falling output prices, the shift in terms of trade against agriculture continues, squeezing profit margins in an already fragile agrarian economy. So is the case with workers engaged in the non-farming sector, with economic activity remaining subdued, particularly in rural construction and manufacturing.

The wages of casual workers in the non-farm sector continue to slide down in real terms.

The net result has been a sharp decline in domestic demand for agricultural commodities, including food and fodder. Unlike previous years, when exports growth made up for deficient domestic demand, the last three years have seen agricultural sector enter a vicious cycle, with low demand leading to declining prices, declining incomes, and wages. The only way this situation can be remedied is by the government intervening to arrest sliding demand.

It is ironic that the farmer is going through the worst phase of misery in the last two decades- not as a result of some natural calamity but because of government apathy.

The government, which promised doubling of farmers' income, continues to be indifferent, blaming the farmer for overproducing and holding him responsible for the collapse of agricultural prices.

Our leaders often make false promises to farmers for their betterment, but all in vain. Government promises for cheap and good-quality seeds, fertilizers, pesticides, etc., to farmers are all gimmicks. They promise to double the price of production of farmers every year, but all proves to be a bluff.

A farmer's life is not full of comfort. His life is full of difficulties and problems. Every day he has to face many troubles to fight against, including climatic disturbances, which are beyond his control. Cyclones, droughts, and unwanted heavy rainfall are like enemies to them. He always prays to God for help. Such inevitable acts of God or nature are unpredictable for farmers.

The Ministry of agriculture had, in July last year, also issued a gazette notification announcing the setting up of a committee in this regard. The notification said the committee would suggest measures to make MSP available to farmers across the country, promote natural farming, and prepare a comprehensive strategy for crop diversification, among other things.

Just five kilometers from Parliament, thousands of farmers wearing turbans of different colours and styles gathered at the iconic Ramlila Maidan on Monday, demanding that the government fulfill the written commitment it made to them in December 2021. The farmers have converged under the banner of Samyukta Kisan Morcha, a grouping of farmers' unions that led around a year-long agitation at Delhi's borders and forced the government to withdraw the farm laws.

The farmers' demands include a legal guarantee on the minimum support price (MSP), withdrawal of cases registered against farmers, compensation to families of farmers who died during the protest, pension, debt waiver, and withdrawal of the electricity bill.

The central government has failed to meet the demands of farmers despite a written commitment.

Thousands of cases against farmers remain pending. More than 750 farmers lost their lives during the protest, and compensation to their families remains unpaid. There are also several other demands that have not been met.

In a statement issued on Sunday, the Morcha had said that SKM leaders would speak about the impact of government policies on farmers, agricultural and migrant labour, the rising cost of living, and declining purchasing power.

While announcing the repeal of three farm laws in November 2021, Prime Minister Narendra Modi promised to set up a committee to suggest measures to make MSP available to farmers across the country.

The Ministry of Agriculture had also issued a gazette notification in July of the previous year, announcing the establishment of a committee for this purpose.

The notification stated that the committee would suggest measures to make MSP available to farmers nationwide, promote natural farming, and prepare a comprehensive strategy for crop diversification, among other tasks.

The centre had also outlined three points for the members of the SKM. The Morcha, however, had rejected the committee, stating that there was no mention of making MSP a legal guarantee in the committee's agenda.

Each year, the central government announces a minimum support price (MSP) for 22 agricultural crops and a fair and remunerative price (FRP) for sugarcane. This is intended to ensure that farmers growing these crops receive a minimum price for their produce. However, the government is not obligated to purchase all the crops at the declared MSP.

Farmers cannot demand the MSP as a right, as there is no legal or statutory backing for this.

The crops that the government procures from farmers in significant amounts include rice, wheat, and cotton.

Public procurement stabilities prices, with MSP acting as a benchmark for private buyers.

The Indian central government introduced three agricultural reform bills in June 2020. These bills, known collectively as the farm laws, were passed by the Indian Parliament at the end of September.

Significant changes in the laws included:

1. Relaxing restrictions on the purchase and sale of farm produce in state-regulated markets, called mandis.
2. Loosening restrictions on the stocking and movement of food items classified as "essential commodities," allowing stockpiling.
3. Enabling farmers to enter into direct contract farming agreements with buyers, bypassing mandis and providing local dispute resolution mechanisms.

Opposition figures and protesting farmers complained that there was little consultation over the legislation.

Indian farmers began mass protests against the laws at the end of September 2020. The largest protests centred on the capital, New Delhi. Many farmers in these protests are from the states of Punjab, Haryana and UP, which are major agricultural producers.

On 19th November 2021, after nearly a year of mass protests against the laws, Indian Prime Minister Narendra Modi made a surprise announcement that the government would repeal the farm law.

There are deep-seated structural problems with the Indian agricultural sector. Landholdings are small, and Indian farms are much less productive than those in other countries. Most economists agree that the sector requires reform and greater efficiency.

Farmers face challenging circumstances. A significant number of farmers commit suicide each year, but this is not a new phenomenon. The issues causing farmers distress go much wider than those reforms are trying to tackle, such as access to credit, technology, education, and severe weather.

Protestors are also calling for the minimum support price (MSP) to be preserved and given legal guarantees. The MSP was not part of the three acts. The government has said they will preserve it, but it currently lacks a legislative base.

The Indian Supreme Court suspended the three Acts in January 2021, establishing a panel to review the legislation. This did not satisfy the protestors, who did not believe the panel would listen to their concerns. The panel's work was completed at the end of March 2021, but the recommendations were never published.

The police and government response to the protests has been criticized, including blocking the protestor's entry into Delhi and using water cannons and tear gas.

On 26 January 2021, during the annual parade celebrating India's Republic Day, some protesting farmers using tractors broke through police barricades to storm Delhi's Red Fort complex. Clashes broke out with the police, resulting in the death of one protester and more than 300 policemen being injured.

Leaders of the protests condemned the violence, blaming the chaos on "rogue elements" within an otherwise peaceful march. They stated that they would not call off the protests.

The government defended itself, saying the protestors only represent a small group of farmers, that protestors had used violence against the police, and that the police had used restraint.

Despite the repeal of the laws, many protesting farmers remained camped outside the capital. They stated that they would not end their protests until the government conceded to several demands, including passing a law guaranteeing the MSP mechanism and providing a compensation to the families of farmers who died during the protests. On 9 December 2023, the protestors said they would return home after receiving assurances from the government on these issues. But farmers' leaders said they would hold a review meeting on 15 January 2022 and warned the government that if it didn't fulfill its promises, they may "resume the protests."

The farmers' agitation lasted for more than 9 years. They were on roads Coocking themselves. Living peacefully in deceptive. They sheltered at usually boarder at border at Sonipat district in Haryana. Local farmers provided full support to farmers from Punjab and joined them in agitation too. Haryana farmers provide lots of help regarding food, milk and many other thing to be required by the farmer sitting on Marchas. There was a great example of unity and love among the farmers of different states like Punjab, Haryana and Uttar Pradesh. Lots of common men also contributed by giving charity in form of money, eatables etc. Some gifted tractors, trollies and other useful equipment to the farmers for their help. That was proper example of brotherhood. Lets pray far the farmers who scarified their loves in agitations. No words are there left to describe the sacrifice and atrocities the farmers faced during agitation. May God help the farmers by listening their voices, full of agony.

A farmer in India is a basic unit of India economy. Farming or agriculture is his livelihood. A men strong in build, wearing dhoti and kurta and a big turbon on his head can easily be marked as an Indian farmers. He gets up early in the morning and gets ready for his daily routine. He goes to his field with his buns. He works in his field. His wife and sons assist him. He ploughs the field and sow seeds. He then water them regularly. He is happy when he reaps rich yield and celebrates the occasion.

The Calander of his farming is dependent on the monsoon rains. He get good crop when it rain sufficient and in time. But occasionally, he has to face dry or wet famine when he may lose his entire crop. Then, it becomes difficult to meet both the ends together.

But this gloomy picture of a helpless and weary Indian tamer is changing rapidly. The wave of development has touched him as well. The government has paid heed to his plight and undertaken many farmer- welfare schemes. It has provided good means of transport and communication. It is executing many educational and medical scheme. So the poor and illiterate framers are becoming literate. They are learning good habits of sanitation and vaccination.

Good seeds and fertilizers are available to the farmers. He can get good fodder for his cattles. The banks have reached the villages. So loan facilities are also available so that farmer can use modern farming equipments than the traditional ones. He can raise a gober gas plant. He can raise an irrigation system for a sure water supply. Government of India is supporting and encouraging agriculture by broadcasting programs on radio and even TV, enlightening the farmers. The recent GAT contract has opened the world wide market for agricultural outputs and products to the farmers. The Indian farmers also are welcoming these news changes and developments in farming. They are taking benefits from them and changing their traditional ways of farming. An Indian farmer is becoming move thoughtful and experiment in his farming. He doesn't prefer to take out the same crops for years together. He now tries different crops. The need concept of 'natural farming' is a revolution and a born for the farmer. The countries like Isreal also are giving co-operation to Indian farmers.

Now a days due to vast deforestation, the Indian farmers have to face grave problems like scanty rains, erosion of soil, decrease in underground water level etc. Government is trying to find firm solutions for these problems. Thus an Indian farmer can no longer be pictured as a poor, illiterate villager. The rapid development in agriculture has assured him bright future and good standard of living so that we may say "The prosperous India can be discovered in its village."

The Indian farmer celebrates the social function in the simplest manner possible. He celebrate a lot of festivals round the year. He celebrates the wedding of his children. But his children's marriages depen on his agricultures yield. He entertains his kith and kin and friends and neigbours. He goes to visit his relations, he attends the open air dramas and songs, and the folk-dances in his locality.

The condition of the Indian farmers should be improved. He should be taught the modern methods of farming. He should be made literate so, might schools should be opened for them, he should be assisted by the government in all possible ways. Because upon well being, depends the welfare of India and its people.

The government must take initiatives for agriculture and farmers. Don't hammer after merely capitalism. Consider the miserable conditions of farmers as well. Make a strong nexus between businessmen and farmers; a proper bond between both is more important for the nation's development. They are two arms of Bharat Mata. Working with both hands will strengthen the country in every aspect, including economy, infrastructure, and other developments. By shaking hands, both farmers and capitalists will make our country rich and prosperous, and the day will come when India will be the richest country in the world. India will once again become a powerful nation.

The financing of the agricultural sector has traditionally been a major topic of economic analysis, with the availability of capital in general and the credit costs for farmers in particular at the centre of research. Since the agricultural sector plays a major role in the economic development of the country, inefficiencies in the supply of capital could have major repercussions not only on agricultural production and food supply but also on the growth of the economy as a whole.

There is a long tradition of government intervention in agriculture for a broad rarity of reasons and compared to an unspoiled allocation of resources with basically two outcomes: protecting agriculture or taxing agriculture, where as the latter is true for many developing countries trying to increase government revenue and/or protecting consumers, governments in industrial countries subsidize agricultural products to increase farm income and food self-sufficiency or-more recently-for conserving the country side. Due to this widespread intervention in agricultural product and factor markets, it is difficult to find empirical support for 'underinvestment' in agriculture which would be the consequence of the theoretically discussed market failure in agricultural financial markets and to separate instrument targeted on failures of financial markets from other interventions which all theoretically not well founded.

One undisputed role of government is to address market failures associated with public goods, externalities, and monopoly power. However, the informational deficiencies discussed earlier extend beyond these conventional problems, where economists have ample experience in suggesting remedies. Since governments generally lack superior information, the type and intensity of state intervention that could be suggested is not straightforward. What seems to be particularly important is the implementation of institutions that allow markets to work, such as contractual arrangements and legal enforcement.

Such remedies are necessary for the agricultural community and their market. Well-planned markets with proper roads and transportation can help farmers sell their goods on time. But again, the prices of farmers' products must be fair and satisfactory for them.

Industrial development and progressive infrastructure are very important for capitalism, but no one can overlook the equal importance of agriculture. All the basic raw materials come from agriculture. Without the support of agriculture, companies and factories can't survive. Agriculture and industrialization are two sides of the same coin. They cannot be separated. So, for overall development, the government must take care of both agriculture and industries.

If agriculture is sound and progressive, then industries will rise simultaneously. Money is needed in both sectors. It is government's duty to address their needs and requirements equally. The government provides huge loans to big businessmen, but these people never repay them. Many big businessmen leave the country without paying their debts to banks. Meanwhile, if any common man or farmer takes a loan from banks and is unable to pay it back for valid reasons, the banks begin harassing them and pressuring them to pay immediately. Under such pressure, a farmer or a common man may even commit suicide. That's the irony of fate. This is our country, where the rich get more money from banks and become richer, while a poor farmer or a common person grows poorer. Why this discrimination? If we want to raise our country, we must support all the communities, whether a rich or poor.

What we need is not market fundamentalism, but a market that functions freely, within the board parameters set by well-crafted laws. The Indian government should repeal its new farm laws and, through a careful deliberative process, craft legislation that stands the test of reason and can benefit poor farmers and consumers most of all.

Agriculture is an intricate issue that raises important questions not just for India, but for all economics struggling to strike a balance between the market and the state.

The corrupt nexus between the sugar industry and governments affects farmers. India is the second-largest producer of sugar in the world, after Brazil.

If there is one crop that affects India's economy, water supply, and promote nepotism, it is sugarcane. India was the first country in the world where sugarcane farming began, and the first refined sugar was produced more than 2000 years ago. In fact, the word 'sugar' has its origins in Sanskrit, 'Shaakara'.

Most of Brazil's sugar is exported, while a large ethanol fuel lobby promotes growth, creating a cruel, paradoxical situation on India. Farmers, who were encouraged by their political masters to farm sugarcane, are now facing an existential crises.

Sugar mill owners owe them almost Rs. 24,000 crore. As a result, farmers are throwing away sugarcane or burning it in the streets to express their protest. The sugar industry engages around 50 million farmers and two million milk workers. Ironically, India imports sugar even though the country is producing a surplus.

Caught in this situation are helpless sugarcane farmers. Despite loans given to the sugar industry by the government, farmers have not been paid. They face a precarious situation. Timing the harvest is crucial, as sugarcane begins to spoil after a few days. So, they are forced to sell at throwaway prices or simply discard the crop.

Significantly, most of the people working on sugarcane farms are migrant workers, as farmers often depend on hiring migrants who accept lower wages and make fewer demands on working conditions. Delays in procurement or government decisions on procurement prices are exacerbating farmer's distress.

Agriculture is not merely a subject of farming; it is now a complete industry. Agriculture consists of many aspects. It is not limited to grain farming; it's scope is vast. It includes vegetable farming, floriculture, medicinal plants, spices, cotton, sugarcane, and fodder, among others. Even rubber comes from rubber plants. Even now a wood is also grown by the farmers such as sandal wood, teck sheesham, rose plants for rose wood, popular plants for paper etc. In this way, agriculture plays a large role in the production of raw materials.

Forestation is also a form of farming. The government takes care of forests. Government keeps check on deforestation and its assets. Government has made forest department for forests to keep constant check on outer interference and our intruders. In forest areas, there are many tress of valuable costs. So, they are being protected by the forest officials. Forest departments keep check on animal poaching from the forests. Illegal trafficking and poaching laws are there for forest wild animals. Killing, poaching, maiming, poisoning or torturing an animal is a cognizable offence.

The reason behind the continued wildlife exploitation is that corruption, weak laws, inefficient judicial systems, and light sentences allow criminal networks to plunder wildlife with little regard for the consequences. These factors make illegal wildlife trade a low-risk, business with high-returns. All animals and birds are part of our natural world; it is our responsibility to care for, protect, and safeguard them.

As mentioned earlier, forests are also a form of farming. The difference that forest are almighty's farming, while others are human-driven. So, we must take care of our forest and their assets. Forests help in rainfall, protect us from floods, and provide wood for fuel, especially for the villagers living near them. Fresh air and many other valuable resources are gifts from our forests.

Please pay attention to the agriculture sector, which provides many essential resources for all other sectors and in all spheres of life. Agriculture can be developed once farmers become prosperous. It's crucial to upgrade the income of farmers. The government must support farmers with kindness.

We all come from farming communities, sooner or later. We are all children of the soil. Everything we receive from Mother Earth. Farmer works hard to provide grains, vegetables, fruits, etc. for every person the earth. But he himself never gets for himself. He is not greedy. He distributes his produce to poor without expecting anything in return. He never asks for money or favours from these poor people. Can any person on Earth distribute their production as charity to others?

The days when rich people did much charity are now gone. Ratan Tata, one of the biggest businessmen in India, donates 51% of his profits for the welfare of our country. Ghanshyam Das Birla denoted extensively to society and built many educational institutions for the youth. Seth Chhajurani, a great farmer and cotton and jute magnate, encouraged village youth to pursue education. He built Jat school and Jat college at Hisar. Sir Chhotu Ram, a son of farmer, devoted his life to the welfare of farmers and helped them to uplift themselves, becoming self-respecting and self-reliant. There are many such examples.

Ch. Bahagphool Singh, a son of a farmer and former patwari, contributed greated for the upliftment of girls' education. Bhagat Phool Singh was a???????????????(page 122). He donated all his land and launched Gurukul in 1936 in Rohtak district. It began with just three girls seeking education, but now around 8000 girls receive education in various fields. Bhagat ji was assassinated by three Muslims on 14th August 1942. After his death, his elder daughter, Smt. Shubhani Ji, took charge of the

Gurukul and expanded her father's vision by expending Gurukul into a big educational institution in North India.

Under Shubhashmi ji's hard work and the blessings of her father, Bhagphool Singh ji, Gurukul progressed daily. With the passage of him and by the grace of God, the Gurukul became Bhagat Phool Singh Mahila Vishwavidyalaya (BPSMV). It was done by strenuous efforts made by shubhasni ji. A great help came from Sh. Bhupender Singh Hooda, when he came first time Chief Minister of Haryana. Before becoming C.M., when it was just a common she was tormented by Chief Minsiter Chautala. Subhashni ji asked for help from Hooda ji and asked to make a university in my of her father BhagatPhool Singh for women. Hooda gave his words and when he came in power to proved his worth by declaring Gurukul as a women university. But, by that time subhashi ji had died. But her drams come took and desires fulfilled.

In this way, there was a time when people worked for the upliftment of the society, especially farmer communities. Those days seem to be gone now. No one is willing to help the society or poor people in the country.

Today's businessmen, like Adani and Ambani, are simply minting money for themselves and not contributing to social or educational causes. This reflects their priorities to amass money for their families, no doubt, but they also have surplus money could help others. The only differences is in mentality.

Farmers need support for their betterment. Instead of grabbing their lands or purchasing them with money, consider that once fertile agricultural land is converted into concrete jungles, would it be possible for us eat food. For food, agriculture land is essential and farmers must be in good conditions. Without food, can anyone survive—either poor or rich? So, it's humble request to the government to think about agriculture and farmers.

Our country needs both the rich and farmers. Everyone has a right to progress. Industrialists are growing rapidly, while farmers are left behind in terms of progress. Why such a disparity? What is the reason? Think. The government must study the entire scenario. A proper balancing is needed.

Farmers are the backbone of Indian society. This is a sensitive issue that requires careful handling. Although they are the backbone of the economy, they still face many challenges, which not only affect them but also broader society. Farmers feed the entire nation, yet they often can't even afford two square meals for themselves and their families.

Additionally, farmers contribute around 17% to the country's economy, but they continue to live in poverty. They are self-employed, depending on farming as their primary, and often their only, occupation.

The Smart Growth Panel faces a difficult task. To respond to the mandate of 'steering growth pressures away from significant agricultural lands', a strategy that is both rigorous and flexible is required. Rigorous measures are needed to withstand the considerable pressures on agricultural land and the agricultural community. Flexibility is necessary to create an environment where farmers can operate successfully.

Traditional agriculture is an extractive process, where all resources-human, water, land—are used for immediate gain. Modern agriculture, on the other hand, uses planned technology and emphasizes conservation practices and the renewability of resources.

The agricultural sector is vital for the region. It is undergoing a transitions to a market economy, with substantial changes in the social, legal, structural, and productive systems, just as in other sectors of the economy.

To summarize, reforms in India's agriculture are mandatory for economic and farmer's advancement. However, these reforms will succeed only when all the factors provide their maximum effort, including the state, the central government, farmers and the mediators etc.

Lastly, but not at ease, over again it pray to all for heling farmers and try to understand his plight of conditions. Let us join hands to uplift farmers. When farmer prosper, India prospers. Let us invigorate the strength of farmers by helping them with fair returns. Capital support will be the greatest form support.

The main objective of the book is to assess the state of the farming community of the country. The relevant areas covered are the level of living of farming households, as measured by consumer expenditure, their income and assets, their indebtedness, farming practices and preferences, resources availability, awareness of technological developments, and access to modern technology in the field of agriculture. Farming households are defined as those households that are engaged in farming activities, which include cultivation of field or horticulture crops, growing of trees or plants such as rubber, cashew, coconut, papers, coffee, tea etc. Animal husbandry, bee keeping, vermiculture, and sericulture etc. are past of farming.

Some disturbing facts about the farming sector include the dissatisfaction of farmers with their profession, their ignorance of about matters most important for their future, and the dismal failure of government, cooperatives, and other agencies in fulfill their tasks.

It comes out first that the general levels of literacy among farmer household are slightly lower than of the overall rural population.

Farming has not been profitable from the very beginning. This indicates that large farmers need more credit and larger amounts of finance for production and social ceremonies. It is a matter of concern that, despite all efforts made for their development, institutional finance and non-institutional sources like moneylenders and traders still provide limited credit. A more serious matter is the failure of the cooperatives in extending credit to farmers. The primary purpose of loans is marriages and other social ceremonies.

To sum up, an analysis of the incidence of indebtedness among formers' households reveals that a majority of them were in debt, and that a very large proportion of their debt sourced from non-institutional lenders. The rates of interest charged by these non-institutional sources are very high.

There was once a time when landholding was relatively high and satisfactory. But today, it is a major problem and a growing concern that the size of landholdings is decreasing day by day and even decimating in some parts of the country. The major reasons for this are urbanization and commercialization. Many construction projects and expansion of factories and companies are acquiring agriculture land by offering farmers big amount of money. Due to population galore, landholding within families are reducing to small plots. In this way, our fertile land is vanishing, and our farmers are becoming landless rapidly. Even deforestation is being caused by lots of infrastructure expansion, such as road building and urbanization. Forests have been razed to make space for development projects like agricultural land.

These are significant differences in income earned by different sizes of landholdings. As expected, farmers with larger holdings have substantially higher incomes than those with marginal and small holdings. Another important difference is that smallholders earn proportionately more from wages, whereas large farmers earn more from cultivation.

For farmer households engaged in animal farming, the only worthwhile and profitable activity is dairying, with some success in piggery and poultry farming. Farming of fishery and other livestock and fishery turns to be a loss making proposition.

While diesel and electricity are extensively used in some states, most farmers in underdeveloped areas continue to depend on bullock power as the main source of energy for ploughing, harvesting, and threshing. For irrigation, the main source of energy is electricity, though both are expensive for farmers. Natural resources such as rivers, ponds, and other natural water channels are scarce, and if they are, they are not maintained and tough to get in used.

It is shame that farmers have a dismal state of awareness and knowledge about themselves. The agricultural sector is in a serious crisis, and a vast majority of small and marginal farmer households in most states are struggling to make ends meet.

The incidence of indebtedness, low consumption expenditure, and the prevalence of poverty and malnutrition are all manifestations of the fact that a large majority of farmers' households are unable to earn adequate amount to meet their bare consumption needs.

The main reason many farmers are unable to earn enough to meet their consumption and investment needs is low productivity.

Small and marginal farmers, as well as landless labourers, should also be involved in deriving benefits of increased agricultural exports through innovative institutions like integrated co-operatives like the mother dairy, and other service co-operatives, contract farming etc.

There is a need for important institutional reforms, like consolidation of landholdings and other land reforms. The first priority should be to give homestead land to landless labourers. This land should be used for dairying by small farmers. By giving homesteads to landless labourers, a large number of marginal farmers could increase their income, which would also boost the dairy industry. Steps should be taken to liberalise the lease market. Furthermore, no action should be taken to dilute legislation on landholding ceilings. In a country where small and marginal farmers constitute above 80% of the landholders, weakening these laws would endanger their only source of livelihood.

I am concerned about the prevailing crisis in the agrarian sector and the poor conditions of small and marginal farmers in most states. The biggest challenge for policymakers is to revive the growth of Indian agriculture, thereby improving the productivity and income of a vast majority of farmer households and agricultural labourers dependent on it.

Our human population is still growing at about two percent per year. Although our farmers, supported by scientists and policymakers, have been able to keep the rate of growth of food production above population growth over the last two decades, crop yields are now stagnating. Affirmative actions can improve the productivity growth in agriculture.

Due to erratic rainfall, even with adequate monsoons, and the intermittent and extensive incidence of floods, cyclones, and near-drought conditions in several parts of the country, extensive damages to crops occurs, hamstringing accelerations of crop productivity thresholds.

Without technological innovations, the potential for higher growth is limited and soon gets exhausted. To maintain a tempo of higher huge investment in new technology are essential. Without investment in irrigation, roads, electrification, and other infrastructure, as well as research, development, and extension services, large increases in agriculture output cannot be achieved.

The agricultural sector is constantly buffeted by the vagaries of weather, the winds of the market forces in terms of plenty and the willfulness of levies and procurement in times of difficulty. Yet farmers have produced more, demanded little, and stoically accepted their growing impoverishment.

The imperatives of our political economy have long demanded that food prices remain among the lowest in the world. It is our inflation-protected, and dearness-allowance-linked urban. both white and blue collared, middle classes that have most benefited from this situation. As a result, a perpetual clerkdom in a government department or undertaking is far more rewarding than the kulakdom, the life of a large farmer with maximum irrigated areas.

Recent economic investigations tend to support the contention that all is not well with agriculture and farmers. While the share of traders and the marketing costs has gone up appreciably, the producers' share of the consumer rupee has gradually declined. This is attributed to the increased pace of industrialization and migration of small and marginal farmers to cities after realizing that farming is less profitable proposition than other enterprises.

Farming in fertile areas like Punjab and Haryana is no longer profitable, largely because of fragmented landholdings.

Agriculture credit, historically, has been the domain of moneylenders. Even after 75 years of independence, the last resort for farmers in many villages remains the institution of moneylenders. The rural credit system is caught in a web-like situation where the farmers have no trust in the banks, whom they view as unfriendly. Rural credit managers often treats every loan seeker as a potential defaulter. During the present times, when liberalization and freedom absolutely curtailed. He has been left to the mercy of a designated bank which will dictate its own terms. An entrepreneur or businessman in the city may take a meagre loan, and that too after lot of palm greasing and humiliation. So, where is the opportunity for farmers to enjoy the marked competitiveness, or to exercise his choice for a better service oriented credit institutional source?

The way the Land Acquisition Act has operated so far has always worked against poor landowners. Large land areas are acquired for irrigation, power projects, roads, factories, and city expansion. When land is acquired in the catchment of a river to be submerged by the construction of a dam, a large number of cultivators are deprived of their means of livelihood so that people living downstream in the command area may benefit through irrigation and become prosperous. That the displaced people are ruined for life and for generations, pauperized through loss of their land, does not enter anyone's calculations. The acquisition of land must be for a public purpose, not for any particular person, party, or private company. There should be laws to prevent private acquisition. In tribal areas, state governments must negotiate with tribes and buy land because they do not have power to compulsorily acquire it. This is a salutary check on the unbridled power of the state to acquire the land of tribals.

The poor, illiterate, and over-exploited women agricultural labourers, running into millions, are an invisible force hardly finding a niche either in official statistics or welfare legislation. Women belonging to this measure ill-organised work force slog their lives all day long without a whimper, for they treat the different chores of farming as an integral part of their family enterprise in the same spirit as they daily grind of house hold work of cooking carrying water and fuel wood or looking after the large brood of children. Come that way, be it the scorching sun, the scudding rain, or the chilly breezes of the long bleak winter, they are these transplanting in the knee-deep water filled rice fields, or attending to odd jobs on the farm all alone or along with their menfolk off the farm too the peasant women can be seen processing, winnowing, trading and marketing the product and this kind of scenario is not peculiar to India alone.

The nation should ensure an enabling political, social, and economic environment designed to create the best conditions for the eradication of poverty and durable peace, based on the full and equal participation of women and men.

The poorer the household, the greater the burden on women, who strive to augment the family income through long hours of labour at low wages.

Rural India has certain unique features that are absent in most other populations worldwide. The majority of the Indian population lives in rural areas, produces most of the food, and yet remains almost invisible to the rest of the world and to the rest of India. While we may see films about rural India and read about it, but how many of us have experienced it to any great measure? Rural India remains largely as it was a thousand years ago, with its undemanding simplicity, its tradition values—such as simple occupation i.e. agriculture—and its near-complete isolation from urban existence.

Poverty, lack of education, and inadequate healthcare have been some of the major sufferings of the rural poor. The problem of rural poverty is not an isolated phenomenon; it is closely linked with the continuation of caste, landlessness, and the absence of land reforms. What is needed is a concerted drive for land reforms, land to the tiller, and social and economic upliftment.

India is a rich country of poor people. Its resources are so vast that a Canadian, having seen our rivers, remarked that if they were in Canada, they could feed three times the population of the world. Mineral resources, forest resources, land resources, human resources, and a variety of other gifts of nature are so immense that we should be the most prosperous people on earth. The tragedy is that we are a country of paradoxes; the richest of the rich live here, as do the poorest; the most enlightened, as well as the most ignorant; saints, savants, and sages, alongside the most superstitious; top scientists and technologists, alongside the most unskilled labour; highly advanced, civilized citizens, alongside tribal aboriginals; the wonders of the world, and the most exquisite pieces of art exist here but also the ugliest spots of wretched slums. India is a country of contrasts, believe it or not.

It is a matter of great pride that we live in such a country, but we hang our heads in shame when we know it inside out. This is because India is clothed in a gorgeous dress, but its body within suffers from the cancers of poverty, hunger, inertia, and superstition. These diseases affect mostly our rural folk. How best to remove these diseases should be the concern of all.

There must be a radical change in our thinking, attitude, behaviour, and character. Awareness of the real conditions in rural India and a sense of empathy for their misery may, at some stage, lead to actions aimed to mitigating the distance.

Mass education is absolutely essential. Education is not merely knowledge but also the ability to face life's challenges. Women's literacy would surely lead to family planning. Our womenfolk would realize that they are more than mere childbearing and bread-baking machines. Our farmers would refuse to be exploited by middlemen, moneylenders, and self-centered leaders. Education is one single Aladdin's lamp that has the potential to work magic in rural India.

As far as rural poverty is concerned, the convergence process seems broadly to have been working, with the coefficient of variation on a declining trend. Thereafter, the process seems to have reversed itself, with the divergence process taking over.

Farmers are making news in a different and tragic way. Dozens of them, mainly in Andhra Pradesh, Karnataka, and Maharashtra but scattered throughout India, poor people hovering on the margins between being labourers and cultivators, dreaming of a decent life with the help of irrigation and cash crops but caught in grimmer realities of dry-land agriculture, are swallowing pesticides. The suicides that sparked the uproar were those of cotton farmers who killed themselves after borrowing heavily, over-investing in inputs, and experiencing crop failure. They are mostly small farmers, owning one to three acres of land.

Beginning with the swallowing of pesticides by cotton farmers in Andhra Pradesh, however, suicides have gained widespread publicity and have come to symbolize the farmers' plight.

It is infinitely worse in the villages, where even on non-load shedding days, lights regularly go dim and flicker in the mornings and evenings, or there are inexplicable and recuring power failures. Worst of all, power surges often burn out the engines that farmers have invested in. Almost everywhere, the crises in power supply is leading factor causing despair and anger among farmers.

Suicides have not been limited to the poor, dry areas. About 90 percent of farmers have to take loans to carry out agricultural operations. Most farmers fail to repay the loan amount due to poor and insufficient yields.

The factors that led to the spate of suicides include crop failure, the inability of farmers to cope with changes in the environment, a poor monsoon, unseasonal rains that followed it, pest attacks on crops, frustration with the failure of pesticides, and, above all, debt.

Agriculture department officials would like to see the entire farming community under the umbrella of crop insurance.

There has been a wave of suicides among farming communities in Maharashtra following a crisis in the agricultural economy of Vidarbha and a few other regions. The State Government seems to attribute this entirely to crop failure due to erratic monsoon, natural calamities, and a pest attack. But, as most of those who committed suicide in Vidarbha were cotton cultivations, and as the economy of cotton cultivation is becoming increasingly vulnerable, it could well be that the caprices of the rain God and the havoc wrought by the American bollworm were merely the last straw.

Unless a farmer had money saved up, they would have had to go outside ambit of institutional finance for their remaining requirements. The commercial banks have more stringent criteria for creditworthiness than co-operative banks.

There is another constraint to the availability of institutional finance. Ordinarily, a farmer who defaults on repayments is not entitled to fresh crop loans. Farmers who are unable to repay the crop loans they took last year have the option of converting their loans into medium-term loans so that they may escape the taint of default and qualify for fresh crop loans. But except for those with holdings of less than 2 hectares, they would love to part-service last year's crop loan of qualify. A large number of farmers in the state do not have the wherewithal for this.

The number of deaths in the plains of Uttar Pradesh, Uttrakhand, Bihar, West Bengal, and in northeastern states has been considerably higher than the number of victims of an entire year's terrorist violence in Jammu and Kashmir. Sadly, however, there are no apparent signs of a serious resolve to address the causes of the calamity. For years, experts have pointed to the growing intensity of floods in the Ganges basin and along the Brahmaputra. The disruption of natural drainage by ill-planned development, human encroachment of floodplains, deforestation in the Himalayas, and poor maintenance of flood control structures have all been cited as reasons for the ravage by the rivers year after year. That expert warnings have not been heeded is quite evident, as the flood havoc has been the worst in a decade.

The destruction of embankments in eastern UP worsened the impact of the floods. Zamindari bandhs, as these embankments are called locally, have been in existence for several decades The eastern areas, from Bihar through West Bengal into Assam, have also been badly affected by floods. All major rivers in these states have become sources of death and destruction. The swelling waters of the Brahmaputra and its major tributaries submerged many villagers in upper and lower Assam, rendering millions of people homeless.

The calamitous flood situation has led to endless discussions year after year on the need to address the problem, but nothing worthwhile has come out of them.

Unlike China, where large numbers of People's Liberation Army and civilian personnel are rapidly deployed to deal with floods, India has no organized, nationwide disaster management program, although each year a promise is made to put such system in place. Our Army Jawans always help people in any kind of disaster or natural calamity. They are the real sons of Mother India. In fact, there are two real sons of Mother India: one is farmer who feeds everyone, and other is the soldier who protects our borders and civilians. Well said a slogan by our Late Prime Minsiter Lal Bahadur Shastri ji, "Jai Jawan, Jai Kissan."

Famine and drought are also major problems for farmers, but there are some kinds of man-made famines. While food is available at exorbitant prices, people lose their purchasing power due to denial policies. Fishermen, especially, lose their livelihood due to boat denial and the ban on use of Japanese nets. The mortality rate among them was very high during the famine.

The denial of justice, coupled with the greed of black marketers, led to the hoarding of food on an unprecedented scale, and there was not much food available in the rural markets. When it was available, the price skyrocketed. Scarcity was artificially created, and it was not the question of loss of purchasing power. No amount of rural employment could have been sufficient to cope with this inflation. We must launch a project of job generation on a war footing to fight poverty and famines, most of which are man-made.

Motivation may be provided to farmers in drought-prone areas to adopt water and soil conservation measures, afforestation, and pasteurization of barren lands. Water harvesting tanks and devices may be subsidized. Research may be undertaken on small on-farm reservoirs. Soil scientists should be encouraged to work on methods for moisture conservation and extension.

On the pattern of food buffer stocks, a national seed buffer for untreated seeds may also be built up. This buffer could be used for consumption or become part of the food buffer if there is no natural calamity. Reserves of short-duration fodder seeds may also be maintained to mitigate the hardships cattle face in case of natural calamities. Changes in cropping patterns may be implemented in contingency of rain failure.

Value-adding enterprises should be organized in a way that more relief funds are spent on material components and building institutional capacities, rather than on providing concurrent relief.

Resources for children and women's development should be largely spent on those left behind by migrants who had to leave their hearts and homes in search of employment or for grazing their cattle. Raw materials for handlooms, crafts, and skills should be provided to such women as drought relief.

Although famine is still prevalent throughout the world, the ability of countries to import food and the efforts of international relief organizations have lessened the effects of famine.

Most thresher accidents occur during the night. The working conditions imposed at odd hours, particularly at night or early hours is common. Causal labourers are more prone to exploitation and likely to work under forced conditions, making them easy victims. There have been several cases where farmhands were under the influence of liquor or opium to enable them to work at odd hours.

The adverse environmental impact of intensive agricultural practices has become a matter of serious concern. Emigration by the menfolk has placed the enormous burden of sustaining hill agriculture on women, who find little support. They are often neglected and outrightly rejected by many agricultural development organizations.

Commercial agriculture is spreading fast, securing tremendous income for farmers, but it has also led to reduced agro-biodiversity and the loss of genetic diversity in agricultural commodities.

It is not the resilience of hill farmers that is lacking. The real gap has been in the development and expansion of critical support services, and the transfer of knowledge and skills from laboratories to the land.

In the 21st century, ecological access to food may become the most important challenge due to the damage presently being caused to land, water, flora, and fauna.

Ensuring food security may remain an unaccomplished dream unless issues such as poverty and population are simultaneously addressed. In such a situation, it must be ensured that ecology and conservation do not work against the interests of the poor as we move towards the sustainability of our agriculture.

The main problem facing farmers is getting remunerative prices for agricultural products. Farmers have no control over the market mechanism. The income of an average dryland farmer owning about two acres of land is not more than Rs. 10,000 a year, which does not include wages of his family members and is less than two months' salary of a clerk in a bank or government office.

There is no doubt that the official attitude toward farmers will have to undergo a sea change. The organised worker is improving his lot at the expense of the farmer. Decreases in the cost of living index are welcomed as decreases in the inflation rate, but in reality, they refledct less earning for farmers.

Support prices, as a rule, are far below the actual market prices. Studies of this phenomenon have shown that in the case of many commodities, the support prices are less than the actual market prices of the same commodities. The least the establishment can do is to try to protect the lowest market price of a commodity from the last season as its support price. In such a mechanism, farmers may still lose because of the increase in the cost of production. But even then, there may be a semblance of justice.

We stand at the crossroads where human consumption has desecrated the land, battered the seas, and chipped away at the very equilibrium of nature, threatening to destroy mankind's only means of survival at the cusp of a new millennium.

At the beginning of this century, humanity began life on an earth where about 50 percent of its ancient forests were still intact. Though far from pristine, it was a world of rolling seas and oceans of land masses teeming with all kinds of life. Vast expanses of wild land were sparsely populated by original humans who knew how to draw sustenance from nature's bounties. Things are different today. The equilibrium has been cleaved.

Urban problems worsen by the day. Several megacities have already surpassed their limits to accommodate the influx of a growing humanity. Such pressure on urban facilities has exceeded a city's tolerance threshold permanently.

In the field of agriculture and productivity, mercifully just in time, two promising trends are emerging—one based on ancient wisdom and the other on modern wizardry. The first employs traditional and sometimes forgotten farming techniques to practice what is called "sustainable agriculture," growing enough food with organic nutrients rather than chemical fertilizer, without exhausting the land.

The Specter of a freshwater crisis that can lead to millions of people being denied access to safe water supply looms over India. The freshwater demand for agriculture, industry, and fast-growing urban centers is expected to double in the coming years.

Agriculture is the only area, or you could say the only field, where prices are decided by individuals other than the producers themselves. Agricultural prices are determined more on other ground, than considering relevant economic parameters of inputs. Prices announced for agricultural commodities are dictated by traders, and contactors, leading to the near fleecing of the producers. The commission on agricultural costs and prices should include interest on fixed capital, like land, loans for crops cultivation, and land revenue, as items of expenditure while reckoning the prices. There is no point in claiming that such items fuel inflation affecting consumers' interest. Though such items are not expenditure in real terms, but because of exorbitant cost of capital base (i.e. land), and that too, when land becomes basic input in production process, there is no reason to exclude it while computing administered prices.

In the present system of computation of cost of cultivation, one important factor which we have left out is managerial renumeration. An agricultural farm cannot survive on its own. Seeds, fertilizers, bullocks, machines, water, human labour, land, and the market, by themselves, do not produce agricultural commodities. There must be someone to coordinate all these activities, devoting full time to arrange for labour, going to banks for securing finances, plant seeds on time, for regulating water and sell the produce in the market, among another tasks. We should compute managerial renumeration, while arriving at cost of cultivation for agricultural prices.

The general argument for crop failures is that crop insurance should take place and address this phenomenon. But where is the needed crop insurance system in India? Is it based on insurance for individual farmers? How can we help millions of farmers with small holdings? Until crop insurance covers all farmers on an individual basis, the risk factors for natural calamities should be considered while fixing remunerative prices.

Although, we do account rent paid for leased in land. But, in most of the cases, it bears little relations to the actual rents paid. So, actual rents prevailing in the market should be computed to protect small peasants. The rental value of own land is not included in the breakdown of the costs of cultivation. When land values in industry or trade are taken into consideration for calculating costs of production, why not apply the same yardstick to agricultural land?

Gandhi ji had proclaimed, "True democracy cannot be made to work by twenty men sitting at the centre. It has to be worked from below by the people of every village. If India's villages were not revitalized, Gandhi ji prophesied, India would perish. If things at the village level were rotten, all work done at the top or at the intermediate level was bound to fall ultimately."

In his approach to rural development, Gandhi ji gave the \utmost importance to eliminating the city-village divide, and ending the exploitation of the villages by the cities, which he described as the worst form of organized violence. The draining of resources from villages to cities must stop. Gandhi ji advocated for radical decentralization and the liberation of India's villages from urban exploitation.

At the doorstep of the new century, agriculture's cup of woes really runs a decade; crop yields in the deuttend of the green revolution have plateaued or are declining; critical rural infrastructures such as roads, godowns, cold stores etc. is far short of demand; the lack of a comprehensive crop insurance system led to a spate of farmer suicide following selective crop failure.

At the most, in the future, agriculture growth must be managed in a more participatory mode. Involvement of people in activities like tree planting, contour bunding, construction of small storage, levelling and reshaping of land, construction of field channels and control of grazing are few of many steps.

Farming is still a big gamble as it is largely dependent on the monsoons. All kinds of risks dominate farmers' lives, and insulating them against these risks is important if the lives of farmers must be improved. A comprehensive insurance scheme must be devised, under which farmers taking loans will have to compulsorily take out an insurance policy.

The government must ensure that the forthcoming agriculture policy emphasis increasing the productivity of agricultural products and reducing post-harvest losses.

The farm sector, besides being a source of all kind of raw material supply to industries, tends to support rural folk by offering gainful employment for most part of the year. Unlike industries, where the basic inputs are unlimited in supply to a large extent, given the capital stock, agriculture continues to suffer from the ills of land degradation and natural calamities. The primary input—land—remains inelastic in supply, and water, another source commodity, playing truant on the production cycle. When these basic inputs act as constraints on the production function of agricultural, the terms of trade for agriculture are quite unfavourably juxtaposed with industries as one finds from sector being shortchanged in favour of industry. Agriculture is the only sector where prices of inputs are decided by people other than the producers himself. Agricultural prices are decided more on political ground than with any consideration of the economic parameters of the inputs involved.

Poverty is not just about whether one can afford a bundle of goods but also what prevents one from doing so. Being poor in India means lacking access to good food, healthcare, and the skills to make the most of economic opportunities. About half of the poor belong to scheduled caste or tribes, living on the fringes of village, and are often landless. Being poor also means a very high chance of being illiterate.

The other crucial implement is land reform, which helps blunt the sharp edge of rural poverty. Even the smallest piece of homestead land gives the poor with security for a lifetime, not the millions of dollars the country uses on producing and importing defense equipment. Every jet fighter takes away the right of millions of children to attend school. A fraction of what is invested in fighting AIDS could be spent on family planning, education, and primary healthcare to help prevent the deadening scourge. To fight poverty, it's time India gets its priorities right. A dollar more for the poor man is worth more than a dollar less for the rich.

The government may give new thrust to agriculture and agro-based industries, as the economy is still predominantly agrarian, with seventy percent of the population dependent on agriculture. Coordinated action by the concerned ministries is required to boost agricultural development and agro exports, helping the government realise its objectives.

Our country will not become truly great unless its tiniest and remotest areas throbs with development. This will not happen unless we educate millions of our illiterate countrymen, who would step into the next millennium blinded by ignorance and crippled by poverty.

Today, about half of our population is illiterate. Education in our country, at all levels, suffers from serious issues like poor infrastructure, lack of dedication among teachers and students, outdated syllabi, high dropout rates, malpractice, and more. Let us seek answers to these three questions: What is the state of education in our country? How is education related to development? What should we do to give fillip to education and make it more effective?

Thus, before talking about economic development, we must first talk about education. More importantly, we must act on it. Doing the opposite would be like putting the proverbial cart before the horse.

If one takes a broad look at today's Indian village scene, a single important factor—the basic flaw—leading to all the chaos and extreme poverty is the lack of resources, finance, and knowledge. This seems to be the crucial error. The broken promise to impart primary education to all eligible children has sadly yet to be fulfilled.

Reforms aimed at improving terms of trade for agriculture, as well as opening up new opportunities for production and trade, will provide incentives for greater private investment in augmenting agricultural infrastructure. They will also provide incentives for making agriculture competitive through the adoption of cost-reducing technologies.

Reforms need to focus on depoliticizing and de-bureaucratising the management by involving farmers, so that a link can be established between the efficiency of the services delivered and the charges to be collected for the services rendered.

The strategy for poverty alleviation and human development, through the expansion of employment opportunities, provision of primary and skill education, and health services, must be revamped by involving the Panchayat Raj institutions. This will help in achieving food security as well as relieving pressure on common property resources.

Mahatma Gandhi's concern for our villages was truly heartfelt. It is evident in the following lines from a letter he wrote to Pt. Jawaharlal Nehru in 1945:

"My ideal village still exists only in my imagination. In this village of my dreams, the villager will not be dull, but will be all aware. He will not live like an animal in filth and darkness. Men and women will live in freedom, prepared to face the whole world. There will be no plague, no cholera, and no smallpox. Nobody will be allowed to be idle or to wallow in luxury. Everyone will have to do physical labour."

Upon reflection, it is astounding to find the striking relevance Gandhi ji's thoughts on villages bear to the hard realities confronting rural India today. Gandhi ji's idea of rural development was holistic. He wanted villages to have an all-round development, which would include physical, mental as well as spiritual dimensions.

The increase in population size, shrinking arable land resources, soil degradation, depletion of nutrients, poor water management and unsustainable use of groundwater, loss of momentum in the growth of food output, inefficient biological utilization of the nutrients consumed due to poor environment, resulting in growth retardation, emergence of diet- related chronic diseases and many more are some of the major problems the country have to face in the long run towards elimination of hunger and malnutrition.

The economy is not in the pink of health, the Finance Ministry admits, but pins hopes on the feel-good factors for a turnaround. It expects the good monsoon to result in higher crop output and a consequent decline in prices of primary products. The government is keeping tight control over the money supply and its total borrowing to check inflationary pressures, accordingly to the economic situation report.

The world is losing its forests, and fast. Three-quarters of the earth's landmass were once covered with forests. Half of those forests have been destroyed or converted to other uses, with the bulk of the destruction occurring since the beginning of the industrial revolution. Of the remaining forests, over half are badly degraded and seriously fragmented. Only one-fifth of the original forest cover remains healthy and intact.

All countries in the Himalayan region should unite and work for preservation or the bio-cultural diversity of the Himalayas, and also arrest the pollution of its physical and cultural environment.

Scholars from the seven Himalayan countries should collaborate as a think tank and find the solutions to the problems linked with pollution, global warming, and the thinning of the ozone layer.

Why do people shoot animals? For food, for profit, for trophies, or for the thrill of killing? Traditionally, in India, hunting has been a privilege of aristocracy. Others also hunted, but mainly for food. As long as man haunted for food, he was just another predator in the ecosystem. When he started killing for trophies, out of commercial motives, trouble began. The arrival of the gun tilted the balance against the animals.

It was during the British Raj that hunting assumed enormous proportions. To break the monotony of their lives, the British took to hunting in a big way. The broon Sahibs and Indian princes copied their master. It was given a respectable name of "sport," and the animal shot were called "game". Hunting acquired a snob value, much like golf.

In the seventies, the hunting lobby was quite articulate. How can we stop hunting? What is the way out? How can we save what little of wildlife is left from these poachers? Villagers around forests sanctuaries can be given incentives to report poaching.

The Forest Department can work in cooperation with the non-government organisations to keep a watch. And if someone is caught, the case should be pursued with vigour so that an example is set. Even now, under certain situations, one can get a licence to shoot boars and ducks. This provision should also be removed, so that there is no excuse to hold a weapon.

Hunting holds a deep attraction for those in position of power. Hunting is means to display power over animal victims and privilege over other humans. Given the important role of hunting in Indian history, it is unsurprising that the age of ecology has not purged this distasteful legacy from Indian culture.

In the past, the hunt was a surrogate for war. It seemed natural a person who could wield bow and arrow, matchlock, or spear against wild creatures would be skilled on the field of battle. Such a destructive cult.

There is a need to learn creatively from the traditions of harmony embodied by peoples like the Bishnoi.

Urban air pollution is only one small part of the damage being inflicted upon the environment in India. Much of our land, air, water, and forests are threatened and in a state of decay and degradation. Forest cover is down to just 11 percent of the land area, or only a third of the minimum desirable level. More than half our land is no longer fertile and self-regenerating. Fifty percent of our land is degraded. Half our rivers have turned into sewers. Piles of green and blue plastic bags choke our water sources. Our ground water aquifers are getting poisoned. People's access to natural resources is rapidly decreasing. Very little is being done to slow down, halt, or reverse the damage. Most ameliorative measures are poor palliative, for example, "compensatory afforestation" for the loss of prime, virgin tropical rainforests.

Despite a blatant environmental degradation witnessed all around, the valuation of products and services and national income has failed to reflect the deterioration.

The future of our agriculture depends on the efficiency of small farm holdings, and if we are to drive maximum benefit out of them, we must solve the problems of the small farmers. Against this backdrop, there are two issues that confront the agriculture scientists. One is adopting the productivity path and facing the problem of increasing biotic and biotic stress on the production process. The other is the over-exploitation of water resources, especially groundwater.

The only realistic way to ensure higher wages is to increase the demand for farm labour by creating more irrigated lands. Minor and medium irrigation schemes, apart from having a salutary effort on the environment, also serve a vital economic and social function by creating employment opportunities in a cost-effective manner.

The small size of land holdings makes it difficult for small and marginal farmers, who belong to economically underprivileged sections of society, to access technical know-how, physical inputs, and other resources.

In the present times, when liberalization and freedom are being granted to the industries and businesses, a farmer feels his freedom absolutely curtailed. He is left at the mercy of a designated bank, which dictates its own terms. An entrepreneur or businessman from the city may take hefty loan on a small plot of land or any other small property by applying all manipulations. A farmer has to mortgager or deposit the papers of this entire land in the bank to take meagre loan, and that too hinges after lot of palm greasing and facing humiliation. So where is the opportunity for a farmer to enjoy the market competitiveness, or exercise his choice for a better service-oriented credit institutional source?

Efforts to raise exports have met with limited success for the simple reason that the full potential of the farming sector has been neglected. The real export effort needs to be based on the unlimited potential of the farming sector. Unfortunately, precious little has been done to tap this potential through appropriate measures.

Certain policy measures are still needed to ensure efficient and productive management of agricultural resources.

But today, in present-day India, while the entire world is progressing swiftly, we are also trying to escalate in every field of progress and development. But we are lacking far behind in agriculture and farmers' development. The pace is slow, and the government is not paying heed towards farmers plight and their atrocities. Government policies are adamant and are not in favour of farmers. While people are just making huge norms which are null and void for farmers those people sitting in air condition rooms are not in cognizant of real problems of farmers on ground level.

There was farmers' protest in 2020-201. The 2020-21 India farmers' protest was a protest against three farm acts that were passed by the Parliament of India in September 2020. The acts, often called the farm bills, had been described as 'anti-farmer laws' by most of the farmer unions, and politicians from the opposition who said that it would leave farmers at the "mercy of corporates." The protests were largely nonviolent. The protest also demanded the creation of a minimum support price bill, to ensure that corporates cannot control the prices. The union government, however, maintained that the laws would make it effortless for farmers to sell their produce directly to big buyers, and stated that the protests are based on misinformation. Related endemic legacy issues include farmer suicides and law farmer incomes. Despite India being largely self-sufficient in food grain production and having welfare schemes, hunger and nutrition remain serious issues, with India ranking as one of the worst countries in the world for food security.

Soon after the acts were introduced, farmers' unions began holding local protests, mostly in Punjab state. After two months of protests, farmers' union, mainly from Punjab and neighbouring Haryana and Uttar Pradesh, began a movement named 'Dilli Chalo,' where thousands of farmers marched towards the nation capital. The Indian government ordered the police and law enforcement of various states to stop the protests using water cannons, batons, and tear gas to prevent them entering Haryana and Delhi. November 2020 saw a nationwide general strike in support of the farmers, with thousands converging at various border points on the way to Delhi.

Smaller but richer states like Haryana and Punjab, with large surplus food production, are the major provider of food security to India as they provide 70-90% of wheat and 29-44% of rice of India's total PDS. Hence, farm reform is more sensitive issue in these food-surplus states with negative food security such as BIMARU states.

On 19th November 2021, the union government decided to repeal the bills, and both houses of Parliament passed the farm laws Repeal Bill, 2021, on 29th November. Following the announcement of the repeal, farmer unions continued with the demand for guaranteed minimum support prices (MSPs), reminding the government of the aim of doubling farmers' income by 2022.

Thousands of farmers from across India have blocked major highways leading to Delhi from 26th November 2020, causing widespread disruption in traffic movement and supplies of essential commodities. These farmers demanded repealing the three farm laws passed by the Parliament in September 2020. Five rounds of negotiations between 40 farmer unions and the central government of India (CGOI) remained inconclusive. The unions were not ready to accept anything but repealing the three laws and rejected the amendments proposed by the Central Government of India.

The Supreme Court of India heard three petitions regarding the agitation on 16th December 2020. The first petition, filed by a law student, demanded the removal of farmers from the borders of Delhi to a fixed place allotted by the CGOI, saying that the roadblocks were hampering emergency and medical services. The second petition pleaded the Supreme court of direct the CGOI to consider the demands of the farmers. The third petition, filed by the farmer unions, sought scrapping of the laws, claiming these laws were arbitrary, and were passed without adequate discussion.

The three controversial farm laws are:

1. The Farmers Produce Trade and Commerce (Promotion and Facilitation) Act, 2020.
2. The Farmers (Empowerment and Protection) Agreement on Assurance and Farm Service Act, 2020.
3. The Essential commodities (Amendment) Act, 2020

Modi ji has announced repealing these three farm law, it's worth taking a quick look at why they had triggered vociferous protests all around. And let us also understand why farmers are not going to end their protest.

Described as much-awaited reforms by the Modi government, these laws allow farmer to sell their harvest directly to private players and enter into contract farming with private companies. Before these laws, farmers could sell their produce only at government-run agricultural produce market committee markets through middlemen. The Essential Commodities (Amendment) Act, 2020, allows traders to stock essential food items, which was hitherto illegal.

Farmers fear that the farm sector reforms could lead to the abolishment of the Minimum Support Price (MSP) regime and end the APMC markets. Under the MSP regime, the government buys farm produce at a predetermined price. The

MSP ensures that farmers are guaranteed a certain price, irrespective of the constraints of demand and supply. Farmers have been demanding a law to ensure the purchase of farm produce at the MSP. They also want the government to abolish the amendments to the Electricity Act.

The new laws open new avenues for farmers to sell their produce, but farmer feared that the new avenues could weaken demand in the traditional APMC markets and force them to sell at prices below the MSP.

Farmers also fear that it would lead to the corporatization of agriculture and eventually push them out of farming. The sale of farm produce would be bound by contracts, thereby making the MSP regime ineffective, they argue. The law allowed farmers to enter into a direct agreement with the buyer before the sowing season and sell their produce at the price agreed at the time of signing the contract.

Farmer fear that the removal of stock limits on food items would lead to indiscriminate stocking by big corporate house which could eventually manipulate the markets.

Farmers now demand a law to ensure the purchase of farm produce at MSP, which they insist was an integral part of the current agitation. They also want the withdrawal of the penal clause to the law related to curbing the practice of stubble burning, which causes air pollution in parts of North India, particularly the National Capital Region, during winter.

The government will now have to move separate bills in the Lok Sabha to repeal the laws. It could just allow the repeal of the bills without any discussion. If the opposition insists on a debate, the winter session will witness a round of government bashing, which the treasury benches will have to bear as they have agreed to repeal the laws.

What is indicated by all these laws and above bills? According to me, they are a kind of process to tighten the grip of government on farmer's rights. A few business tycoons and politicians want to suffocate the farmer community. In fact, they are trying to trample these farmers under their gigantic feet.

You know one thing that at the time of covid the entire world was at the mode of standstill due to lockdown. Everyone was confined to their houses. No work done. Business came to halt. There was no movement and everything paused. All kind of business, factories, manufactures, retail came under the effect of lockdown. Even big business tycoons were in devastating conditions because they faced lots of loss. The economy of entire world darted down like arrow. Even in our country the same scenario was there. Our economy also get affected, but still India was moving ahead gradually. You know how? Our economy no doubt also came down but still we were having 4 to 5% economy due to our agriculture. Every trade and business came to halt where as our farmers kept on working hard and did not allow our country to get hungry. Our farmers provided everything related to farming like every kind of grains, vegetables, milk and poultry product and due their toil and dedication, we had food to survive and even our country could survive with some reliable economy. Salute to our farmers and their endless efforts.

"No farmer, No food"

Upon seeing this, certain politicians and business tycoon's start pondering that agriculture is the only profession that can go throughout time, regardless of conditions. However, they forget that agriculture is humanity's first profession. Without agriculture, no one can survive. From food to raw materials, everything come from agriculture. The base of entire economy is agriculture. I don't disparage the entire business class for development, but still the backbone of our economy is agriculture. So, please do not ignore it—respect farming and the farmers. They are the foundation of the nation, and if you are try to undermine the foundation, you will fall and won't be able to survive.

This is sensitive topic that needs to be landed carefully. The people of India are engaged in variety of profession, agriculture or farming is the main occupation in India. In contrast, though they are the backbone of the economy, they are facing many problems that not only affect them but also other people. Although farmers feed the entire nation sometimes, they can't even afford two square meals for their families.

Before the 1970s, India was not self-sufficient in producing food grains and imported a large sum of food grains from other countries. But when our imports started blackmailing us then Prime Minister Sh. Lal Bahadur Shastri ji find an alternative and motivated our farmers. In addition, he gave a slogan, "Jai Jawan Jai Kisan," which is still remembered to this day.

After this, the green revolution started in India and we became self-sufficient in food grains. Moreover, we started exporting our surplus to other countries.

Besides, farmers contribute around 17% to the country's economy. But still, they live their lives in poverty. Also, they are self-employed and depend solely on farming as their primary and often only occupation.

Farmers feed the entire nation, but they themselves struggle for two square meals a day. In addition, many are committing suicide due to debts and burden of guilt that they can't feed and provide a prosperous life to their families. Many farmers are migrating to cities to find a move stable source of income that can provide a proper food supply.

If the rate of farmers suicides and migration continues, India may once again become a food importer rather than exporter. Due to large scale campaigning and the issue of farmer's suicide is highlighter. But are these efforts enough to save our Annadata (food provider a farmer) that the question which we should ask our self?

The persistence of the problem can be judged by the fact that every year, hundreds, even thousands, of farmer commit suicide. The main reason for their suicides are the repayment of loans which they are unable to repay due to various reasons. In addition, the maximum number of farmers are forced to live below the poverty line. Above all, they are forced to sell their produce at lower costs than the MSP.

In conclusion, we have passed a long way since independence but still, we need to do a lot. The villagers and farmers still after doing this much for the economy still spend there in misery. But, if we take the matter seriously and try to resolve the problems of farmers then soon a day will come to the villages will become prosperous as the cities.

The condition of Indian farmers is dire. Around 80% of the farming population own less than 1 hectare land or between 1 and 3 hectares. Agriculture provides employment to nearly 50% of the population, but still contributes only 15% to the GDP.

Small farmers are vital to India's agriculture. These farmers, who own 2 or less than 2 hectares of land, constitute around 70 to 80% of the total farmers of the country.

The farmers had to bear the cost of indigo farming, and the British planters used to keep the yields without compensating the farmers. Not only this, but they were also exploited through lots of restrictions and norms. Farmers have been neglected both by the Britishers and as well as by we people. It is a shame on our society and our nation. The person who feeds us, sleeping with empty stomach. It is an irony of fate, created by man-made circumstances.

For me, farmers are an embodiment of God. They are epitome of strength, willpower, dedication, and kindness.

The role of the Food Corporation of India (FCI) is not only to deliver rations but also to instill confidence in farmers by bringing transparency, efficiency, and accountability, Union Commerce, food and consumer. FCI should emerge as a trusted partner of farmers and the people of the country. The FCI plays a crucial role in facilitating flagship schemes such as Pradhan Mantri Garib Kalyan Anna Yojna (PMGKAY) by providing ration to beneficiaries in every corner of the country. FCI should embrace digitization and technology to improve efficiency. Quality can be achieved in areas such as inspection, procurement, transportation, distribution, and storage.

FCI must reduce operational costs through route optimization, mechanized loading/unloading, innovative storage solutions, and other methods.

The Open Market Sale Scheme (Domestic) has also proven to be an effective tool in moderating the prices of wheat and rice.

India's self-sufficiency in food, which ensures that no citizen in the world's most populous country sleeps hungry, is one of the greatest achievements in human history.

The corporation, which runs the government's granaries, must continue winning the trust of farmers through transparency in its operations, adopt more digital technologies to achieve high quality and explore ways to keep its expenses under limit. The statutory organization has been critical to maintaining the country's food security, as it buys millions of tonnes of farm produce from cultivators at federally fixed minimum support prices (MSP), a process known as procurement. It than redistributes the food to 850 million poor people free of cost under the National Food Security Act. MSP is a floor price to help avoid distress sale by agriculturists.

At an event marked by diverse cultural performances, I acknowledged the role of former Prime Minister Lal Bahadur Shastri in setting up the federal food agency.

Buying food from farmers and distributing it to the poor helps to strengthen every child through food security.

The government is providing lots of schemes for farmers and their produce. No doubt, certain steps have been taken in this direction by government, but still there many who sleep with empty stomachs. Yes, the major reason is our large population. But, apart of all such kind of hurdles, we must ponder over such issued and more and effective steps to be taken to curb hunger.

Second major problem, and the most dangerous, is corruption in our society and government agencies. To achieve positive results, we must eradicate corruption from our country. Strict actions should be taken against corrupt officers, politicians, or anyone who engaged in such hypocrisy.

Certain steps must be taken to uplift the standard of farmers. First, there must be proper and firm connection between farmers and the government officers. Government officers must come forward to help farmers in every situation, regarding agricultural latest research on farming irrigation, manure, cultivation, pesticides and, last but not least, the proper and effective markets with reasonable prices of their produce. A strong bond between the farmers and government will lead both to the pinnacle of their development and progress.

Second, farming must be considered a business. By doing so, then check all prospective of farming and first calculate the entire expenditure of farmer doing while entire process of cultivation up to their yield. On calculating entire expenditure, make out reasonable prices of farmer's produce. Farmers' input is much bigger than output. So government must take steps to increase the output of the farmers and provide them profitable prices for their produce.

Third, crop insurance is also very important. Government must persuade farmers to insure their crops, so that they can have reasonable compensation for their damaged crops due to any kind of climate reasons.

Last but not least, education is crucial. Provide education to everyone with minimal cost. Ensure that every citizen in our country is educated, especially the farmers. With the help of education, farmers can understand the ups and downs of the market. They can sharpen their wits and upgrade their conscience. Once they are educated, farmers can go for other options of income. Educated farmer cannot be fooled by anyone. They can easily understand the government policies and make out if the policies are favourable. Due to education, farmers can ponder on every matter and things for their development and progress. An illiterate man is like blind man, pitfalls and misfortunes await him. So education is most important for everyone.

The biggest problem for farmers is finance. In our country, most farmers are in deteriorating and devastating conditions. A large part of our farming community is still poor. Very few are in good condition. Our government must take initiatives and steps to transform these poor farmers to well-beings and wealth. Just imagine, if every farmer becomes rich or is in favourable position, our country will again be known as the "Golden Sparrow." Collective and positive efforts are needed. Poverty must be eradicated at the grassroots level, and you will find that the day is not far when our country will be at the top of the world. Just ponder, then plan, and finally execute with complete transparency.

The typical life of an Indian farmer is full of difficulties and hardships. In spite of his hard labour¸ he survives a life of extreme poverty. He is born in debt, lives in debt, and passes away in debt. His crops are at the mercy of rain and other climatic conditions.

Farmers are the backbone of Indian society and as well as Indian economy. Also, this is a sensitive topic that needs to be handed carefully. The people of India are engaged in a variety of profession but agriculture or farming is the main occupation in India. In contrast, though they are the backbone of the economy still they are facing many problems that not only affect them but also other people. Although farmers feed the entire nation sometimes they can't even afford two square meals for them and their families.

Before the 1970s, India was not self-sufficient in producing food grains and imports a large sum of food grains from other countries. But when our Prime Minister Sh. Lal Bahadur Shastri ji find an alternative and motivated our farmers. In addition, he gave a slogan, "Jai Jawan Jai Kisan" which is still remembered till day.

After this, the green revolution started in India and we became self-sufficient in food grains. Moreover, we started exporting our surplus to other countries.

Besides, the farmers contribute around 17% of the country's economy. But still, they live their lives in poverty. Also, they are self-employed and depend only on farming as their main and only occupation.

Farmers are the driving force of the economy. That's why; a major sum of our population is directly or indirectly involved in it. Furthermore, every citizen of the country is dependent on the agriculture products produced by them.

Farmers are committing suicide because of the debts and burden of guilt that they can't feed and provide a prosperous life to their families. Many of the farmers are migrating to cities to find a more stable source of income that can provide their family with a proper food supply. But this leads to lots of problems like some are being attracted towards crime, some go far begging, some become labourers and some even, specially their woman are being caught in the web of sex business. Such an irony of fate. May God help these poor farmers!

But, if the condition of farmers suicide and migration continues that India will again become a food importer rather than exporter. Due to large scale campaigning and the issue of farmer's suicide is highlighter. But are these efforts enough to save our food provider (Annadata) that the question which we should ask our self?

Besides, the relentlessness of the problem could be judged by the fact that energy year hundreds of and thousands of farmer commit suicide. The main reasons for their suicide are the repay due various reasons. In addition, the maximum number of farmers is forced to live below the poverty line. Above all, they are forced to sell their produce at a cost lower than the MSP (Minimum Support Price).

In conclusion, we have passed a long way since independence but still, we need to do a lot. Also, the villagers and farmers and villagers till after doing this much for the economy still spend there in misery. But if we take the matter seriously and try to resolve the problems of farmers then soon a day will come to the villages will become prosperous as the cities.

The condition of Indian farmers is very poor. Around 80 percent of the farmer's population consist of those farmers who own less than one hectare land or one to two hectare. Besides, agriculture provides employment to nearly 50% but still contributes 15% to the GDP.

Small farmers are vital for India's agriculture. These are the farmers that own 2 or less than 2 hectares of land. In addition, they constitute around 70%- 80% of the total farmers of the country.

The Indian farmer grows crops not just for his own family but for all the families of our country. He works hard on the farms in all kinds of weathers. He does not care about his health. His wealth is his crop. He lives a humble life in a small house, and even in huts. At times, he does not even realise the true worth of his grain. He is often cheated by moneylenders and paid a pittance for the grains he sells. If the farmers were to give up their occupations, the people of our country would starve to death. Therefore, we need to realise and acknowledge the importance of the people who feed us.

With over 60% of the population dependent on agriculture for their livelihood, farming is more than just a profession; it's a way of life. For the Indian farmer, every day begins with the first rays of the sun. They rise before dawn, their calloused hands bearing the scars of countless hours spent tilling the land.

A farmer works tirelessly to provide us with the food we need to survive. Despite the hard work, many farmers face challenges such as poor soil quality, lack of access to modern technology, and insufficient government support. Scarcity of water and other natural calamities are major problems farmers face. These challenges have led to widespread poverty and distress among farmers. However, with the help of government initiatives and technology, the situation is gradually improving. Farmers are now able to access better seeds, irrigation, technology, and the financial support. This has led to an increase in crop yields and improved livelihood for many. Climate change, increasing population, and rapid urbanization are also affecting farmers in India. The Indian government and society should take positive steps to address these challenges and support the Indian farmer in order to ensure a sustainable and prosperous future for the farmers and for the country. They Indian farmer is a symbol of resilience and determination, and their contribution to the country must be recognized and celebrated.

One of the major farmers' problems face is the loss of agricultural land. As more land is lost, it becomes increasingly difficult to produce the right volume of food required to feed the entire population.

The agriculture sector plays a significant role in the Indian economy. Around 60% of the total Indian population is engaged in agriculture, contributing about 18% of the country's GDP. Farmers are played by several issues. These directly or indirectly affect the farmer's life. From procurement of inputs to marketing and post-harvest activities, farmers face a lot of challenges. However, the problems faced by farmers go often unnoticed. Here are some of the problems faced by our farmers in India.

1. **SMALL AND FRAGMENTED LAND HOLDINGS:** Indian agriculture is mainly dominated by small and fragmented land holdings. This makes the farmers less competent. Most farmers have marginal and small operational holdings of land. Small and marginal farmers constitute 86.2% of the total operational holdings. Due to this fragmentation of land, farmers do not generate adequate income. This is because of difficulty in mechanization, practicing usual agricultural practices like monocropping and products which lead to deterioration of land quality. This leads to high production costs and low productivity. The root cause of this problem started due to the inheritance law.

2. **LACK OF MARKEING AND STORAGE FACILITIES:** Problems faced by farmers in agricultural marketing include high transportation costs, inadequate market infrastructure, price fluctuations, lack of proper market information, and the role of exploitation

by local traders and middlemen. The lack of storage facilities in rural areas has been a limiting factor for post-harvest losses. Nearly 20 to 25% of grains, fruits, vegetables, oilseeds, pulses and other crops produced are wasted every year due to lack of storage facilities. Since most agricultural produce is perishable, farmers are forced to sell the produce immediately after harvest, even at lower prices. This gives them a meagre income. Insufficient storage facilities make it difficult for the farmers to meet people's demands during the off-season.

3. **POOR ADOPTION OF MECHANIZATION:** Despite the expansion of mechanization in India, most of the agricultural operations are still done by labourers. Although machinery has been developed for seeding, weeding, and other agricultural operations, only few farmers use it for crop production. Due to small land holdings, small farmers find it difficult to adopt mechanization. Lack of awareness among rural farmers and capital constraints create this problem.

4. **CREDIT AVAILABILITY:** In the agriculture sector, availability and access to timely, adequate, and low-cost credit from financial institutions sources are more important, especially for marginal and small farmers. Along with all other inputs, capital is one of the most crucial inputs for increasing agricultural production. Access to credit is one of the factors influencing farm productivity. Farmers facing capital constraints would use fewer inputs by not investing in better technologies, machinery and equipment in their production activities

compared to others having no such constraints. This affects not only productivity but also the produce quality.

Improved credit access may facilitate optional use of inputs and have a major impact on crop productivity. Even though the government is improving agricultural credit policies, regional imbalance in credit distribution persist over the years.

5. **POOR IRRIGATION FACILITIES:** 80% of water consumption in India is for irrigation in agriculture. Depletion of the groundwater table is a major factor affecting agriculture. Good irrigation helps farmers to carry out timely agricultural activities. The steady decline in the groundwater table can be noticed in recent times due to its over-exploitation as 65% of irrigation uses groundwater sources. In India, irrigation facilities are limited, and the majority of farmers are still dependent on rainfall. Rainfed agriculture accounts for about 51% of the net down area in our country and occupies nearly 40% of total production.

6. **SOIL FERTILITY DEPLETION:** After the green revolution in the 1960s, the use of chemical fertilizers increased. To get quicker results, farmers began using fertilizers excessively. Excessive usage of chemical fertilizers contributes to reduce organic matter content and human content, decreased number of beneficial insect, poor growth, increased pest attacks and altering of soil pH which ultimately leads to low productivity. Imbalanced use of area leads to soil fertility depletion over a period of time.

7. **INADEQUATE ACCESS TO CROP INSURANCE SEHEMES:** The major problems with crop insurance schemes faced by farmers include lack of awareness of insurance schemes, evaluation of extend of damages caused due to crop losses, inadequate coverage of insurance schemes and non-payment or delayed settlement of claims.

8. **IMPACT OF CLIMATE CHANGE:** Climate change can lead to changes in weather patterns, such as increased frequency and intensity of extreme weather events like drought, floods, and storms. These changes affect soil fertility, crop yields and livestock production, leading to reduced productivity and income for farmers. Farmers may need to invest more in pest and disease management practices, which increases their costs and reduces profits. Heatwaves can cause heat stress in crops, which affects the yield especially when they occur during pollination, pod or fruit set. Climate change can also lead to water scarcity in some regions, which affects irrigation and reduces yield. Farmers may be forced to rely on rain-fed agriculture, which can be more unpredictable and vulnerable to climate change.

   Unpredictable rainfall affects several agriculture operations, and unexpected rainfall during harvest can lead to total crop loss. Heavy rains that result in flooding can be detrimental to crops and soil.

9. **PRICE VOLATILITY:** Price volatility can significantly impact the livelihoods of farmers, especially small farmers who are more vulnerable to market fluctuations. Price volatility can lead to income

instability as sudden drops in prices reduce their income and profits. This makes it difficult for farmers to plan and invest in their farms, leading to a vicious cycle of poverty and low productivity. This situation creates uncertainly for farmers as they are not sure of the prices they will receive for their produce in the future. This makes it difficult for farmers to make informed decisions about what crops to grow, how much to produce, and when to sell their produce.

10. **POOR TRAINING AND EXTENSION FACILITIES:** Agricultural extension programs help farmers by means of transfer of technology, assisting farmers in problem solving and contributing system in India is not equally balanced. Without adequate training and access to extension services, farmers may not be aware of the latest farming practices, technologies, and techniques that can help them to increase crop yields. This results in reduced yield and, consequently, affects farmers' income.

Lack of training and extension services also makes farmers vulnerable to pests and diseases, leading to reduced yields. Without access to information on how to prevent or mitigate these risks, losses are incurred. Farmers may not have knowledge of recent schemes, financial assistance, and how to access the financial resources to invest and increase their yield due to lack of training and extension activities.

11. **LIMITED SPENDING ON R&D BY THE GOVERNMENT:** Limited government spending on research and development (R&D) negatively

impacts farmers, resulting in reduced productivity, increased costs, and reduce profitability. If government expenses on R&D is limited, then farmers may not have access to new technologies and practices, improved crop varieties, leading to reduced productivity and competitiveness in the market. Government investing less in R&D may force farmers to invest their own resources in adapting to changing conditions which can be expensive. This may increase the production cost, making it difficult for farmers to compete in the marketplace.

The Indian farmer community is comprised mainly of small and marginal farmers who majority face all the above challenges in agriculture. Farmers face a lot of problems in agriculture right from natures' activities to man-made activities, including climate change, soil erosion, biodiversity loss, water, resource depletion. Major cause of these problems adoption of modern technologies, lack of capital or gap between farmers and government institutions. These problems cannot be fully solved but can be mitigated to some extend by following wise agricultural practices, sustainable use of resources and bridging the gap between rural farmers, government and financial institutions.

We must thing about farmers and their atrocities. If the backbone is displace, how will be possible to recuperate the entire losses.

Why do Indian farmers kill themselves? Can anyone help these poor farmers? Can market reforms help? What our government doing for these poor farmers and their atrocities?

In fact, 85% of India's farmers operate less than or just five acres of land half of which in many parts of India may be dry or rainfed. Small farmers contribute 51% of agricultural output with 46% of operated land, and a must higher share of 70% in high value crops, such as vegetables and milk. However, small farmers are less literate and are from marginized caste and communities, and are generally excluded from modern market arrangements, like contract farming or direct purchase.

Many studies show that small farms, or very small landholdings, can produce as much as or higher value of output per unit area than the medium or large farms, which refutes the arguments that small farms cannot be the future of Indian agriculture. Therefore, it is not the size of the farm, but what a farmer does on that farm —when, how, where, why, and how much —which makes it viable or not.

Given the cereal-dominated cropping pattern, farmers can only earn so much from their small farms. Furthermore, only about 50 percent or less of the household income of cultivating farmers comes from farming, with the rest made up of wages, off-farm, and non-farm work. Therefore, non-farm sources of income are suggested to be crucial for small farmer families to escape poverty or even achieve a decent livelihood.

The problem of small farmer livelihoods is aggravated by the fact that small farmers suffer from many production risks, like drought, flood, lack of adequate use of inputs, poor extension leading to large yield gaps, lack of assured and adequate irrigation, crop failure and so on. The production risk coverage, which was being attempted through crop insurance, has not worked well.

Further, there are market risks like absence of market, poor price realization, high transaction cost, and poor bargaining power due to small marketed surplus. This leads to low and unstable form incomes for these producers. It is here that the role of market becomes crucial as even if a farmer has produced efficiently but is not able to sell well, the story is lost. The distress among small farmers in India is therefore market-driven to a large extent, in both ways too much protection (MSP) or too little. Once the farmer takes produce to the mandi, he can't bring it back, much like taking a dead body to the mortuary.

Markets, though important, are only part of the smallholder livelihood problem. Most produce is sold outside the mandis, with only about 1/3rd of the total marketed farm produce going through them. Therefore, the MSP culture, and too much reliance on low value land intensive crops has been the culprit in many suicide prone areas, while high production and market-risk crops like cotton in others. Most problematic issue is the farmer's reliance on traders, commission agents, and non-expanders for credit as institutional credit reaches only 65 percent of them and more of small and marginal farmers are excluded from this institutional credit net. This private-source borrowing leads to interlocking of credit and output markets, where there is implicit overpricing of farm inputs and under-pricing of farm outputs. They offer better prices as they don't offer credit to farmers who are tied to traders and agents.

Further, if smallholders and tenants belong to lower castes, their access to credit may be limited either through complete denial of credit or costly access because of higher rate of interest charged or unfavourable terms of repayment. This makes their farming enterprise unviable.

It is also important to realize that smallholders suffer high market and price fluctuation risk, and institutional mechanisms to address the lacking. The prices are still determined and driven be APMC markets, which remain inadequately regulated and, in many cases, mistreat farmers. Therefore, it is important to ensure fair functioning of such markets in terms of open auctions, proper unloading, storage, and handling of farmer produce, especially perishables, which are generally auctioned from roadsides and fliting grounds. and stopping of commission being charged to farmers even in regulated markets.

What is needed is pre-production and post-production aggregation to buy better, sell better, or capture a higher surplus in the food and fiber value chains.

Majority of farm families sometimes face illness and poverty followed by poor access to resources, low education, decimated finances, and lack of skills.

Small and marginal farm families face small size of land. Majority of families face high labour as their main livelihood problem. Small and marginal farmers are facing many problems to operate the high-risk farming. These risks are related to weather uncertainties, uneven access to technologies, natural resources, unreliable input supplies, stressed infrastructure or irrigation, uncertain marketing arrangements, inefficient water management, lack of access to inputs, lack of timely support, lack of knowledge, lack of ability to diversify, lacking connectivity, lack of access to credit, lack of value addition at farm level and lack of required finance. Due to these limiting factors, the small and marginal farmers suffer from the low productivity, instability in yields, low employment, less income and poor standard of living which are responsible for less bargaining power in input and output marketing of Indian farmers in present economic scenario. The increase in population, subdivision and fragmentation of landholding due to breakdown of joint family system is further resulted in un-economic landholding on which application of new agricultural practices become more difficult. So, the study is conducted with the objective to identify livelihood problems perceived by farm families.

Problems related to livelihood include problems related to agriculture, household, climate, government and markets.

Considering problems-related to household, the majority of farmers always face a lack of capital. Financial constraints impede agricultural production and have a negative impact on livelihood of small and marginal farmers. These constraints include a lack of finances, high cost of inputs, lack of human labour, unstable weather patterns, insufficient land, poor prices from buyers, poor soil, pests and disease, and poor storage.

The study concludes that problems of livelihood faced by majority of farm families are lack of capital, non-availability of improved seeds and fertilizers, crop damage from late heavy rain, timely procurement, lack of skills, and declining soil fertility and underground water.

The families of poor farmers are in devastating conditions. Adequate availability, access, and means to consume enough safe, nutritious food are critical for a healthy, productive life. For millions of people living in poverty throughout country, hunger and malnutrition pose serious threats to their health, wellbeing, and livelihoods every day.

When food is scarce, it has been reported that many women will reduce the amount of food they eat or skip meals entirely to ensure that their partners and children don't go hungry. Hunger and conflict are wholly intertwined. These conflicts are often the main cause of hunger in many of the food crises. Conflict may displace farmers, destroy agricultural assets and food stocks, and disrupt markets and consequently increase prices, which damages livelihoods.

In this vicious cycle, conflict and lack of food break down the very fabric of society.

While women around the country are farmers, they often do not receive the rights and resources that men do. Women are responsible for 60-80% of food production in low and middle income countries and half of the world's food production. Yet, they own less than 10% of the land.

When women are menstruating, pregnant, or lactating, they have greater micronutrient requirements, and adequate protein and energy intake is even more important. During these periods, women also need to consume more calories to support the development of their babies and the production of breast milk. Poor nutrition impacts not only the health of women but also the health of their children.

Certain projects aim to improve smallholder farmers' incomes by increasing the volume of farmer's produce, connecting farmers to buyers, and launching new initiative like kitchen gardens. These small plots of land near people's houses are particularly important for women, enabling them to grow their own produce and maintain an independent source of income and food security.

When women gain economic empowerment, the effects spread across families and communities. Women invest more of their income in family needs such as food, medical care, and schooling, improving opportunities for the next generation.

Millions of people in the developing world have fallen into poverty as a direct consequence of global food and energy prices surges. The impact on poverty rates is drastically faster than the shock of the covid-19 pandemic. The current cost-of-living crisis is expected to hit women the hardest, with persistent pay inequality and undervalued work being the main reasons behind the increased financial load they have to shoulder. Woman are also usually the primary caretakers for children and elderly, and in times of crisis, they are disproportionately pushed out of employment and forced to stay at home. Without sufficient government support, they are often left to struggle alone in increasingly dire conditions.

These difficulties are particularly challenging for rural woman, who face additional hurdles on their way to financial independence and stability. When crisis hits, rural women are hit the hardest, usually due to poor access to resources, services, and information, the heavy burden of unpaid care and domestic work, and discriminatory traditional social norms.

In many regions across the country, farming is the main source of livelihood and an important income source for the rural population.

Rural women, who often struggle to secure their own land to farm in the first place, are facing heightened difficulties in the wake of global crises such as conflict and climate change.

In our country, rural women and girls spend most of their time on unpaid care and domestic work. Traditional gender norms retain a storage hold on people's daily lives in many rural communities, and women are expected to shoulder the majority of household chores and children.

To help achieve the equal distribution of unpaid work and domestic responsibilities, I engage with men, religious and traditional leaders, local authorities, and citizens to ensure political and social recognition of the role of women.

We must recognize that reducing and redistributing the responsibilities of unpaid care work has been highlighted as a priority for women's economic empowerment in our country.

Lack of access to financial, government, and other services is a common obstacle for rural women around the country. Gender inequalities, rooted in discriminatory patriarchal systems and social norms, mean that women are less likely to access agricultural extension services, markets, land, and formal financial services despite their high participation in the agriculture sector.

National and local professional organizations play an important role in rural development, but on their own, they have only made limited progress in addressing the challenges facing rural women. With government support, we can reinforce capacities of rural women to increase their income and access to inputs, knowledge, markets and decent work, while strengthening national institutional capacity to implement laws that facilitate access to financial services and advance women's land rights.

Our country has an economy bound to its historical agricultural tradition. In the north, the Indus valley and Brahmaputra region are critical agricultural areas with water supplied by the Ganges and monsoon reason. Agriculture is a way of life for the majority of India's population. Women are an important but often overlooked population involved in India's agricultural production.

The phrase, "Poor agriculture, poor king, poor country" is often attribute to Thomas Jefferson, one of the founding fathers of the United States and the third President of the United States. Very well said.

The condition of farmers in India is still critical. We are hearing farmer' suicide every week or month. Moreover, farmers are all have been living a difficult life for past years. The problem is that they are not getting enough pay. Since the middlemen get most of the money, farmers get nothing in hand. Moreover, farmers often lack money to send their children to school. Sometimes, the situation gets so worse that they don't even have proper food. Thus, farmers face famine. As a result, they attempt suicides.

Furthermore, the other reason for the worst condition of farmers is global warming. Since global warming is hampering our planet in every way. It effects our farmers too. Because of global warming, there are delay in seasons. Crops get effected. And if the crops are not getting watered properly, they get destroyed. This is one of the main reasons why farmers are getting destroyed. As a result, farmers commit suicide. Farming is a profession which needs hard labour and efforts. Moreover seeing the growing population of our country, we must take initiatives to help farmers of our country.

India has more than 230 million poor people. This refers to individuals who, while not classified as poor, experienced deprivation in many things like food, cooking oil, gas, housing, nutrition, sanitation, schooling, household assets, drinking water, electricity, and child mortality.

India's unemployment rate rose to the highest level in over two years in October 2023, with rural areas experiencing in increase in joblessness.

Majority of crimes are related to cruelty by husbands or relatives, kidnapping, assault, and rape committed against women.

Farmers lost standing crops to excess and untimely rain, leaving to a significant blow to their incomes. Southwest monsoon was below normal and erratic, impacting kharif crop yields in many parts of Jharkhand, which are facing drought and drought-like conditions. Recurring losses due to the pink bollworm pest on the cotton crop in North India added to farmers' distress.

There is an increase in deaths by suicide among those involved in farming. At least one farmer dies by suicide every hour in our country. Deaths by the suicide of agricultural labourers are higher than among farmers or cultivators. The dependence of an average agricultural household for income has been increasing on wages from farming, rather than crop production.

"We don't have anything for lunch and even in the evening, it depends. If we get it, fine. If we don't, we will still sleep. Whenever we wake up, we do not anticipate any meal. On a good day, we have a single meal" – A poor farmer.

The role of women in agriculture is very important and significant. We cannot neglect their pivotal contribution in agriculture.

She is a rural woman who works form daybreak until sundown, often beyond. She may run a small business or cultivate a field, or both, to support her family. Long hours are spend collecting water and fuel and preparing food. She sees to the raising of children. She tends livestock.

Without rural women and girls, rural communities would not function. Yet, women and girls are among the people most likely to be poor, to lack access to assets, education, healthcare, and other essential services, and to be hit hardest by climate change. On almost every measure of development, rural women, because of gender inequalities and discrimination, far worse than rural man.

Our country has committed to upholding the rights of all women and girls. Fulfilling this commitment is particularly urgent in rural areas. Rural women and their organizations are moving forward to claim their rights and improve their livelihoods and well-being.

"Women's right are human rights. But in these troubled times, as our world becomes more unpredictable and chaotic, the rights of women and girls are being reduced restricted, reversed. Empowering women and girls is the only way to protect their rights and make sure they can realize their full potential." –United Nations secretary General, Antonio Guterres.

Around the world, the United Nations system stands behind the realization of the rights of rural women, in principle and practice.

There should be objectives through assisting implementation of national and local programs. These directly engage women and girls in rural areas, supporting their efforts to access all the elements fundamental to their rights and well-being, whether health services, land, financing or climate-smart technologies, among others.

Around entire country, almost a third of women's work is in agriculture. Much is this time-intensive and poorly paid, without the full protection of labour rights. Empowering rural women in agriculture can unlock change on many fronts.

In our country, there is equal ratio of vendors as man and women. The women vendors make a living, but hours are long, profits are often low and conditions difficult. Many come from rural areas and have to sleep at the market for days at a stretch, putting them at high risk of gender based violence, crime and theft. Women vendors have a right to the full range of protection and support measures that can help make their livelihood a decent one.

Gender discrimination can intersect with other disadvantages in rural communities, which often have limited access to services, markets communications, and technology. The combination of these factors makes rural women among these most likely to be left behind.

For many rural women, limited economic opportunities push them to migrate in search of better work and lives. Although migrant women have a diverse array of skills and experience, the continuing demand for domestic and care work in many destination countries means these women often fill such jobs. Many find they are not covered by labour laws or basic social protection measures. Results are that some of the rural women who migrated to urban cities, fall prey to massive problems like poverty, sex crimes, and even forced to be prostitutes by force.

Technology has increasingly become a tool for women farmers to improve their livelihoods. Even a simple use of mobile phones can provide ready access to essential information, such as weather forecasts and market prices, which can help women boost productivity and income. The platform also sends regular text message on new business opportunities agricultural practices and women's rights.

Rural women often have unequal access to land and other productive assets needed for income, food, and well-being. This can open the door to additional forms of discrimination and even violence.

Clean, reliable energy improves health and livelihoods and eases work burdens both inside and outside the home. Mostly rural people still don't have access to electricity. Small-scale, low-cost alternatives, particularly in remote areas and poor communities, can play a vital role in extending power and making energy democracy a reality.

Laws and legal practices must uphold women's equal right to land and women should be equally represented in all collective decisions on using land and natural resources. Rural women must also be able to acquire skills, finance, and technology to make the best use of productive assets. Women organizing together can claim a full spectrum of economic rights, including through steering public policy decisions.

It is time to recognize rural and indigenous women that work the land and produce food for the people.

Rural women are at greater risk of experiencing multiple forms of violence and harmful practices. Violence can occur in homes, places of work, or in public spaces, such as while women and girls collect water or firewood.

In six Indian states, a special education program supported by UN women and a local non-government organization helps women understand their rights to live free from violence and to protect themselves from the scourge of human trafficking.

Higher levels of poverty, limited access to justice, and entrenched discrimination are among many factors that put women and girls in rural areas at increased risk of violence. Rural girls are more likely to become child brides than their urban counterparts throughout country. Girls need to be educated so they can be self-reliant and know how to protect themselves.

The human right to food underpins all other human rights, and is one in which rural women play a major role as they grow and prepare much of the food consumed by their families. Yet food security and nutrition are increasingly understand by industrial agriculture, conflict, and climate-related shocks. Gender discrimination limits rural women's access to food security and nutrition in multiple ways, constraining their access to credit, knowledge, and essential services.

Drought, increasingly severe and common in a changing climate, means much more than water scarcity. For many of the poorest rural women and girls, it requires spending hours a day fetching water instead of on more productive activities. It can lead to higher rates of violence, poverty, hunger and an increased likelihood of dying during childbirth.

Health care for many rural women is out of reach or poor in quality. Privatization can impose additional costs, felt most acutely by the poorest women. Poor health and lack of reproductive rights can compound other deprivations, limiting rural women's and girl's well-being and perpetuating gender inequality.

Education is a Cornerstone of individual and social well-being, shaping informed and productive citizens. It should teach the next generation, both girls and boys, how to read, write, calculate, and properly communicate properly- and how to strive for a more equal word, free of gender discrimination. Schooling should not be interrupted by early marriage or pregnancy or inaccessible due to barriers such as language or location. Moral values and ethics must be the part of education system. Modern education with technology must be introduced and make sure be practiced.

A number of developing countries are now aging at rapid rate and will be old long before they are rich. Among those most vulnerable to poverty in old age are rural women, who are less likely to have sufficient saving and assets to support themselves. Many lives in places where traditional social safety nets, provided by families, are eroding, including through the migration of younger people of cities.

Rural women have the right to well-being at each stage of life, a principal supported by social protection programs that ensure basic income and essential healthcare. Lifelong learning helps an older woman retool their skills, opening continued opportunities for income.

Women play a major and pivotal role in agriculture. Even they work harder than their male counterparts. They are the real combination of Goddesses Lakshmi, Durga, Parvati, Kali and Sita. They are real epitome of love strength, sacrifice, patients, hard work, dedication, wits and emotions. Male and female, wife and husband, are epitome of Ardhnarishwar. Women are strength of men and men are shield to protect their women. Both are intermingled with each other. Marriage couple are having one soul, one body and one life. They are not separated. They are one from the depth of their hearts.

So, if a farmer working hard in his fields, his wife is also contributing with all her efforts. It is a joint venture. Male farmers must understand and realise the contribution of their females counterparts. They must respect them and support them in every conditions.

Farming has been a joint venture between men and women since the beginning. Lots of tales are there, that picturise the contribution of both male and female farmers toil to feed the entire nation, but sleep with diplated stomachaches of their own. They face the music in their lives. Everything is opponent to them -from nature to government. They face the hardship of life by themselves and keep on improving ahead with the regular and strenuous efforts. Their smiling faces do not match with their empty stomach the smile on their faces and palm describe the story of their devastating life. When they breath, the inhale lots of problems. When they look around, they find lots of distress. They bow before God everyday but sleeps with Dissonant. They actually Discontent with their lots. Though they live within the ambit of colourful nature, their lives are in Dark and Dull. Gaiety and prosperity seems to be blurred for them. Farmers work hard for the entire nation and world and produce most important stuff for everyone - 'food', is being neglected or overlooked by the world. This is an irony of their fate that how long they will be humiliated and neglected.

Tribal farmers' income is unstable, which has a negative impact on their livelihood by limiting their access to health, education, housing, employment, savings and investment. Farmers suffers from low income due to low productivity due to less fertile land, less use of manure dependency on monsoon backward technology, and unproductive use of debt. Thus, we see that there are various income and livelihood issues for tribal farmers. All these issues can be shortened if we adopt the bottom-up effect. The bottom-up effect is the way in which the base farmer will be involved in the agricultural development. At the formal level, basic needs will be met with the help of real penetration of funds through banks and other financial institutions. Currently, India's banks and financial institutions contribute almost 36% of the debt on the accounts of tribal farmers. Thus, I try to discuss the income and livelihood issues of tribal farmers in our country also suggest remedies to resolve these issues.

The practice of planting a wide variety of crops by the tribe could hold the key to strengthen climate-smart agriculture in country that has been buffeted by recurrent droughts and erratic rainfall.

"We hear about the stories of farmers committing suicide in different parts of India. But we have never faced such a situation when all are crops are lost and there is no hope for our survival," said one farmer in Orissa.

For indigenous farmers, agriculture is not just about the yield or producing more, but about growing food without harming nature, the soil, or the ecosystem, while creating food opportunities for the many other co-existing species.

Farmers are innocent, yet they are being looted, left with a marginal food for survival.

The progress of the country is tied to tribal development, as a tribal population in our country is significant. The tribal economy is mainly hunting, collecting, and fishing or a combination of hunting, collecting with shifting cultivation. The tribal agriculture is primitive and backward resulting in low productivity. Tribal agriculture is characterized by small landholding, improper land utilization, 4 farming techniques overgrazing of pastures, low capital investment, and low production inputs. Tribal areas are in the nature's lap and agriculture has unique potential to absorb these people and creating opportunities for employment.

It is found that tribal farmers are aware of some improved farming practices, but do not have detailed knowledge and training on method of application of fertilizer (organic and chemical), doses and methods of harvesting, and inter-culturing. Tribal women constitute half of the work force among tribal in our country. Tribal women are discriminated, though they make enormous contributions to the agricultural and allied sectors. Due to absence of employment opportunities in agriculture sector, youth belonging to tribal communities are finding themselves at cross-road of life. There is strong need to sensitize and train the folks through adequate extension, policy and financial support for holistic development of tribals in our country.

Tribal farmers, the Scheduled Tribes are recognised lower classes outside the formal Hindu caste system, were once highly self-reliant, and highly creative but deprived of the benefits of their efforts. Relegated to the bottom of the social structure, tribal families gravitated to remove forest regions of the countryside, the managed a livelihood by farming and utilizing forest resources. British rule, vast side were nationalized and tribal villages became dispossessed and destitute. When the British departed, the Indian government took control of the national forest and treated tribals harshly, as if trespassers on their very lands where their ancestors had lived for ages. One crucial incident helped turn the live. Forest officials were accustomed to destroying tribal crops and structures, confiscating livestock and forcing farmers into road work as punishment. Public out-cry eventually lead to clamour for a recognition of tribal farmers' rights.

Once tribal farmers have secure titles to their lands, their access to credit improves dramatically.

Farmer's poverty has been a global concern, primarily in poorer rather than more efficient areas.

We must not interfere or encroach upon their land and their lives. You must set them free on their communities. These tribal people are quite close to nature and, therefore, understand its importance and value. Tribal villages are in the lap of nature and feel safe. They never try to poke their nose outside of their world. They never distract other people away from their tribes until and unless they are being disturbed first. They don't need any help. If we must help them help them why not disturb them and let them live their own life.

Don't trespass on their land and even think about building certain infrastructure in the name of development. Basically, in the name of development or progress, some builders or companies want to forfeit their land. We must stop all such encroachments and misdeeds. No doubt, tribal land has lots of minerals underneath of earth surface. But once these companies enter these tribal lands, they will destroy the entire greenery. The lifestyle of these tribal farmers will be disturbed and will get affected. Not only will these tribals be affected, even entire human beings will be affected by lots of deforestation and soil erosion. Entire ecosystem will change and we will have to face lots of problems like global warming.

Tribal people or farmers have their own lifestyle. They are closer to nature, so they work according to nature. They use the natural process of farming like they use natural manuring, ploughing with bulls, using animal dung in menuring, and in many other things like cooking, fire making hurts, etc. They collect firewood from forests. They sometimes go hunting in forests for their food. But they never kill animals every time. They make animals pray for their food if needed. Mostly, the prefer fishing because they are in abundance. Actually, nature is their heavenly abode.

Let them use their own farming methods and livelihood. Don't disturb them by forcing modern techniques. Just help them by providing crucial and educational facilities. Don't try to build extra infrastructure like shopping malls or company offices. Let them live their own lives. They are happy within the ambit of nature. In this way, we can save our nature and its resources. We can save our ecosystem. Let our mother earth be green in some of her part otherwise one day will come that we will not find any plantation and will be deprived of oxygen to breathe. Think, it is a question of great concern.

Now let us come back to farming and labour. Over the past two decades, there has been a significant decline in female labour. When compounded with gender bias and caste discrimination, women often find themselves situated at the bottom of the labour pyramid, which limits their employment choices primarily to the agriculture or the formal sector. This has been attributed to economic instability among the lower castes, which pushes women into the labour market.

What I want to explain is how, despite of obstacles rooted in caste and gender bias, women's participation in the workforce has a favourable influence on the socio-economic fabric of society. It not only liberates women from social and economic constraints but also contributes to shaping a more educated and enlightened future. My work on women's labour is a comprehensive exploration of gender and caste dynamics in India's labour market that dives deep into the challenges faced by women, particularly from lower castes.

We have to create more inclusive policies addressing gender and caste disparity in the workforce.

As India throttles to become the fast-growing economy in the coming years, it will have to grow in the wake of global agreement at COP-28 to face on unabated coal and other natural resources. Due to rapidly increasing population and many demands of organization, any future predictions of India's reliance on natural resources are laden with uncertainty. The country has affirmed that while it continues to rapidly expand renewable development, our natural resources will remain a vital energy source till they reach the status of a developed country in a geopolitically turbulent world.

To keep the economy's power, we must use natural resources and its existing assets better, while simultaneously limiting exposure to new resources and investing in resource storage capabilities to integrate a higher share of renewable resources. Proper and accurate use of the natural resources, or we can say minimum use of our natural resources, will prove boon to the future generation in our country.

Back to the farmers. Farming is a major contributor to the economy both in terms of employment and output. In many developing countries is the main source of livelihood for the majority of the population. Ruler development is totally based on farming which the backbone of ruler community.

India is a country of farmers. About 70 to 80 percent of the population is still directly or indirectly dependent on agriculture. That is why a great country like India is known as an agricultural country in the world.

Farmers manage large tracts of land. Their practices have a significant impact on the environment. Sustainable farming practices help to conserve natural resources, reduce Greenhouse gas emissions and protect biodiversity.

Farming is a major contributor of the economy both in terms of employment and output. In many developing countries agriculture is the main source of livelihood for the majority of the population.

Often the backbone of the ruler community. Farmers play a key roll in maintaining vibrant and thriving ruler areas.

Farmers play a significant role in contributing to the Gross Domestic Product (GDP) of India. Agriculture contributes about 40 to 50% to India's GDP. This share was 51% in the 1950 - 1955. But it is gradually decreasing with the progress and development of the country.

Farmers provide food for the country's entire population. Agriculture is the only option for arranging food for this population full stops therefore the supply of food grains to this population of the country it can be completed only by growing intensive agriculture practices, climate and soil-friendly crops and their species. This problem can be solved by growing different type of crops like paddy, wheat, maize, jowar, pulses, oilseeds, etc.

Farming is also a major source of national income. Along with the increase in the income of farmers through crop production, various taxes related to agriculture production such as revenue tax, irrigation tax, production tax, generate income for the state and central government. The nation receives a large amount of foreign exchange from the export of some crops such as tobacco, jute, coffee, sugar, to foreign countries. The maximum share of India's income is obtained from agricultural and related business.

The major industries in our country get the raw materials from agriculture only. Cotton, jute, textile industry, sugar, vegetable plantation industries, are directly dependent on agriculture. Small and cottage industries like Handloom weaving, oil extraction, rise pounding, also get their raw materials from farmers.

About 70% of the total population of our country still lives in the villages and earns its livelihood directly or indirectly from agriculture or its related agriculture industry for its sustenance.

The mechanization of agriculture in India is 40% which is much lower than Brazil's 75% and America's 95%. Due to this, there is a decrease in agriculture productivity.

It is essential to have good Seeds for a good crop. But due to the lack of a proper distribution system, these expensive and good seeds are not accessible to small farmers. Supply of fertilizers is also another problem for the farmers.

Farmers often sell their agricultural produce through brokers, mandis, and commodity communication, who often buy their crops from them at unfair prices. Hence, the farmers do not get the right price for their crops.

Illiteracy among farmers is another hurdle to their development. Most of the farmers are not able to take advantage of the government scheme related to agriculture due to a lack of education.

Landholding is now becoming a major problem to farmers. Due to the increasing population, the portion of the land reduces accordingly. Members' increases in family make reduce the land. The main reason is the vanishing joint family system.

Last but not least, finance is the biggest hurdle in the life of farmers. Most of the population of our farmers are poor. You can say that they are hand-to-mouth. The situation is worse for most of the poor farmers. They do not have proper and sufficient meals to eat in a day.

However, farmers face several challenges that hinder their productivity, profitability and quality of life. But addressing these challenges will help farmers improve their livelihoods and promote sustainable agriculture development in India. But can this help if such challenges are being address to deaf ears of government.

Government and business tycoons, all ignore the problems of farmers and even sometimes push farmers to problems. Rich people take everything from these farmers and give very less in return. They exploit these farmers from the very beginning. Contract farming and bondage labour are the results of exploitation. They never get good food and sound sleep. They are always under lots of debt. Life is becoming hell for them. Try to understand the plight of our farmers. Even god is indifferent with their conditions. Don't know, how and who will listen to their griefs and can we possibly help them.

Farmers have a rich historical contribution in freedom of our country. They play pivotal role in our freedom and sacrifice their lives for our freedom.

India has a rather long history of the farmer movement that has shaped their social and economic conditions to a large extent today. Its origin can be traced back to the colonial era when farmers from across the country mobilised in large members to protest against the atrocities perpetrated against them. They revolted against issues like high tax regime, blatant, exploitation, underpayment, and losing rights over their land. There have been numerous farmer movements, including but not limited to, Champaran (1917), Kheda Satyagrah (1918), Bardoli Satyagrah movement (1925), Tebhaga movement (1946-1947) and Deccan riots (1875). These movements mobilized farmers in the overall nationalist movement that led to India's freedom in 1947.

India was a largely agrarian society when the British occupied the country. Agriculture was not conducted without its problems, but it was sufficient for the sustainability and livelihood of farmers. Around 85% of the population earned their livelihood from agriculture and related sectors using the colonial era.

However, the British wanted to maximize their profits at the expense of farmers and peasants. Farmers had to go through lots of problems like:

1. **The exploitation of agricultural labours:** Zamidar and landlords exploited poor farmers to the point that many even worked as bonded labourers on farms. Their wages were abysmally low, while their working hours were terribly long. They were deprived of basic needs and dignity.

2. **Unfavourable policies:** Colonial rulers carefully devised policies that benefited those poor already privileged. They were men to protect and benefit moneylenders and landlords.

3. **High Taxes:** Tax rates during the colonial era were one of the highest in the world. Even if the farmer's crops failed, they were not exempted from paying taxes. Many sold their children just to keep up with the tax.

4. **Zamidari System:** It was a major impediment to farmers' growth, conditions, and economy. It was prevalent mostly in the Bengal Presidency. Under this system, whatever profits were made on the farm went to the Zamindar's pockets instead of the farmers.

Farmers' movement in the country before the 1900s was unorganized and staggered. One of the most significant movements in this period was the Indigo movement. Here most farmers were forced to grow Indigo instead of food crops to maximize profits. This results in many problems for farmers. They were given meagre prices for Indigo and it's resulted in a fall in soil fertility. It also did not provide food security as farmers could eat Indigo.

The Indigo Commission rule stated that it was illegal to force cultivators to grow Indigo. Farmers emerged victoriously.

Deccan riots of 1875 were held to protect against the high money demand of Marwadi and Gujarati moneylenders. High duties were imposed on farmers and land revenue was increased by 50%. An Indian farmer's meagre income could not afford such heavy duties. Hence, social boycott movement was organized in 1874, in which, they decided to not purchase from their shops and not serve them in any capacity. And cause prevalent in western India, but it could not be entirely successful. However, the government passed Deccan agriculturist rights Act in 1879.

Mahatma Gandhi emerged as a major national leader in the early 20th century. He led the fight for Indian farmer's upliftment. Champaran Satyagrah of 1917 remains a historic movement led by him.

Champaran Satyagrah:

In Bihar Champaran, farmers were horribly exploited. They were not compensated fairly for their work. They were forced to grow Indigo on at least half of their farmland, for which they received minimal income. In 1912, Mahatma Gandhi arrived after returning from South Africa and refused to leave the village until farmer's demands were not met. Champaran Agrarian Act was passed in my 1918, as per which formers for free from pain high taxes. The movement turns violent at the end, which went against Gandhiji's principle of non-violence. Nevertheless, it is considered an important former movement in the freedom struggle.

Kheda Satyagrah (1919): In Gujarati's Kheda, farmers harvest failed due to drought-like conditions. However, even then they were forced to pay taxes, leaders like Gandhiji and Sardar Patel come together to fight for the farmer's cause. The prime demands raised by farmers were fulfilled by the government.

Bardoli Movement (1928):

Even after a crop failure, the British government refused to omit tax collections and hiked the land revenue by 30%. Agitated farmers come together and all attempts by the British forces to suppress the movement failed. In the end, the text payment was omitted for that year and the hike in land revenue was lowered down to 6% only.

Movement in India after the 1900s played a huge role in the overall Nationalist movement. Poor peasants were made aware of their rights and their role in the freedom struggle. They struggled against the unfair tax regimes and policies imposed by the British government. Through non- cooperation and non-violence, they brought the British to their knees, emerging out victorious in the end.

In North India, and across Punjab and Uttar Pradesh, farmers sacrifice their lives for independence. Incidents like Jallianwala Bagh massacre shook the entire country. Many people were killed and wounded. All of these people were farmers or common men. The Jallianwala Bagh massacre, also known as the Amritsar massacre, took place on 13th April at the Jallianwala Bagh in Amritsar, Punjab at the time of British India. The protest was against the Rowlatt Act. In response to the public gathering, the temporary Brigadier General R.H.E. Dyer, rounded the people with the Gurkha and Sikh infantry regiments of the British Indian Army. The Jallianwala Bagh could only be exited from one side, as its other three sides were enclosed by buildings. After blocking the exit with his troops, he ordered them to shoot at the crowd, and continue to fire even as a protesters tried to flee. The troops kept on firing until their ammunition was exhausted. Many people including men, women, infants, kids, old people were killed and wounded. Around 1500 or more work killed and 1200 or more were seriously injured. The crowd of non-violent protesters, along with Baisakhi pilgrims, who had gathered in Jallianwala Bagh in Amritsar were massacred by the British. Almost all these people were farmers.

Likewise, Sardar Bhagat Singh, Rajguru, Sukhdev, Chandrashekhar Azad, and many others sacrificed their lives in the freedom struggle against the British. Throughout India, from Lahore to Deccan in the South, everyone fought for freedom. I don't disparage others, but maximum of sufferers were from villages and the most affected were farmers. There were many people who laid their lives for the independence of our country.

So, describing certain ways agriculture affects our daily life. Think agriculture is not for you? Think again. Every single human being on this planet is dependent on agriculture. There is more to the industry than traditional farming, though it is vital to each of our lives. Here are some ways agriculture affects our everyday life—changes are, you may not have considered a few of them!

'FOOD'

This one's easy to underestimate. You are not just consuming food from a farm when you eat a salad, vegetables, rice, dal, or chapatis. Even the sweeteners in your energy drinks come from the agricultural products.

'FUEL'

You will think about this one the next time you are at the pump. Farmers play a huge role in creating sustainable fuel, thanks to ethanol, a corn-derived oil used in gasoline. And little-known fact is that corn starch is also used in the production of tires.

'TEXTILES'

Every kind of fabric comes from farmers. Stepping on cotton sheets, wearing clothes, leather belts, woolen clothes, and many more are products of farming.

'SPORTS'

Think agriculture is not affecting you while you watch any sports being played in the stadium? Agricultural expertise is required to maintain the turf on the field and to fabricate the hardwoods on a basketball court. Don't forget that footballs, basketballs, and cricket balls are made from animal hides.

'THE ECONOMY'

Our country's economy is agriculturally based economy. Still 17 to 18 percent of the entire economy is based on agriculture.

'PERSONAL CARE PRODUCTS'

Have you ever looked at the ingredients in your toothpaste? It contains orbital, a derivative of corn. Many cosmetics contain agricultural products, including tulsi, Ashwagandha, and many more. Corn derivatives are used in everything from lipsticks to powder, as well as in your shampoo and conditioner. Even milk is used in many cosmetics.

'ENTERTAINMENT'

Avid reader? Or love a game night with friends? Your books, your deck of cards, and your board games are all made from agricultural products. And a glass of wine, cold beer, whiskey, or juice you might be drinking, while you enjoy them? Yes, you can thank a farmer for those too.

As we are describing the importance of farmers, we move forward by shading light on more of their contributions widely.

Farmers are very important part of the agricultural industry. It is undeniable that without farmers the agricultural system of any state will collapse. Agriculture fulfils the need of food as the grown crops can be harvested like wheat, rice, sugarcane and many other and then can be processed further until they are ready to be transported.

None of these things would be possible without farmers, as the growth of healthy crops with reasonable yield requires care which can only be provided by them. Farmers are the central part of society as some of the reasons discussed further below:

1. Agricultural Backbone

Farmers hold the backbone of the agricultural system. For a country to progress, the gross domestic product should be reasonable, and agriculture is one of the important parts. The agricultural system will only run if crops are being grown and harvested, and this is where farmers come in. They help the agricultural sector grow, which not only feeds the local people but also gives the advantage to the economy by exporting the given goods to foreign countries.

For export, the material must be of good quality, which is only possible when farmers are very careful and considerate about the factors influencing crops. By exporting goods to other countries, the economy of the country grows, which can be further spent towards the development of the nation.

2. Grow Food

We may need other professions in our life at a different point in our lives, like if we are sick then we go to a doctor, when we need to learn a skill, we need a mentor. These professions are important, but life without farmers wouldn't be sustainable. We all need farmers every day. For the growth of a sound mind in a sound body, we need proper food.

This food is provided by the natural foods and vegetables grown in crops at different times of year, depending on the seasons. This proves that the importance of farmer is more than with think; we take their efforts and work for granted. We never think twice about the food we have for breakfast, lunch and dinner.

Farmers are responsible for the availability of healthy food at our dining tables three times a day. Some plants like cotton are used to make fabric which is sewn into clothes — indicating that even the clothes we wear have some effort from the farmers in the countryside.

No farmer, no food, no clothes. We will be roaming naked with empty stomachs.

3. Experienced Individual

By spending time in the fields, farmer gain experience and know how to handle different scenarios. They know what to do when the weather becomes unpredictable, how to avoid waterlogging and salinity, and how to remedy the situation.

On-field work makes them more informed and responsive to the issues that need addressing. The more time one spends in a profession, the more he learns. The farmers must plan crops every year, put in fertilizers, and reap the crops when they are ready. The repetitive cycle teaches them which seeds would be better, and which fertilizers would provide more yield.

In the movement of crisis, they know how to minimize the damage to the crops. If there is a fire, they know to cut out a certain amount of crops, even if it is not ripe, so they can disconnect the fire from the bigger part of the field prevent the destruction of the entire field.

4. Durable Assets

One of the reasons we need farmers is because they are capable of withstanding harsh weather. A person from a corporate background is used to sitting in an office and working in an air-conditioned environment. Farmers must grind in the sun making them comparatively resilient to harsh changing weather.

People employed in air-conditioned offices might find it harder to walk out in the sun in summer, or cold breeze in winter, while farmers are backboned by the situation. They know their task is at hand and any negligence will affect the annual yield which can devastate the economy of the country.

If the farmers are unable to perform their duty or show ignorance in their labour, it might result in famine or inflation. The feeling of responsibility helps them work under harsher conditions too, after a while they become used to these conditions, hence and we do require labour under almost any circumstances. One should acknowledge the importance of farmers as they bear these hardships for their nation.

5. Disciplined Worker

Farmers are such people, who go beyond the call of duty to deliver their work, as the weather conditions may change, or the crops might need to be sprayed for insects and pests. They put their soul to their task, as they know their ignorance can cost them the crops which will not only cause the depreciation of the economy but more importantly will be no food for the people.

Farming is not only about planting and harvesting the crops. They must be properly taken care of the entire year and spraying them timely with pesticides to keep the crops from being eaten.

Being cautious if any natural calamity strikes or in case a fire breaks out. They must be on guard for the crops as neglecting their duty might result in loss of year-long hard work in addition to the fatal blow to the economy of a possible famine.

6. Selfless Citizen

While a person in a corporate environment might need incentives and constant reminders to work efficiently, a farmer on the other hand doesn't need huge monetary rewards for his labour. They only need the required resources to grow crops like fertilizers, seeds and materials required to cut the crops in the harvesting season.

Apart from these utilities, farmers do not require much motivation to work as they have as they have enough sense of responsibility on their mind. They know in order to feed their own family and the entire country, they must give their best to the task at hand. This is enough motivation for them to give their best effort and to be causes about their duties.

7. Symbol of Dedication

Farmers are symbols of hard work and dedication, and society can look up to them as a source of inspiration. Farmer's day is a public holiday in some countries on different days. It is celebrated on 23rd December in India.

The main idea of this event is to encourage, motivate, and appreciate the efforts of farmers' communities. On this day, people recognize the efforts and dedication they put in every year. They acknowledged their importance in their lives.

By seeing all the given factors, it can be safely said that farmers are a vital part of our society. They help us to fill our basic needs of food and clothing ourselves. We cannot deny their importance as their efforts make our regular-day-life run smoothly. Help the agricultural sector and farmers of the country.

They are a mark of dedication and preservation as society looks up the source of inspiration. Appreciate their efforts for keeping the society well-fed and the economy blooming. As the saying goes,

"In the winter's chill or the summer's heat, a farmer works so the world can eat."

Farmer is, I think, a God. He releases whatever he is heaving. He fills the stomach of the entire population and sleeps in hunger. Such an irony of fate! The producer of food is without food. I am weeping on seeing such circumstances.

8. Think Twice

For all human beings, the sun, the earth, the moon, water, and everything is very important and we can't think to survive without all of these. The same is with farmers too. Farmers are equally important for us. Without farmers, we cannot have food to eat.

Let us come to the conclusion. The Indian economy is an agro-economy and highly depends on the agricultural sector. Despite, just supporting the Indian economy, the agricultural sector also supports the industrial sector and international trade in import and exports. This is an agriculture.

The agricultural sector is of vital importance for the entire region. It is undergoing a process of transition to a market economy, with substantial changes in the social, legal, structural, productive, and supply set-ups, as is the case with all other sectors of the economy.

Farmers are the backbone of Indian society. Also, this is a sensitive topic that needs to be handled carefully. The people of India are engaged in a variety of professions but agriculture or farming is the main occupation in India. In contrast, though they are the backbone of the economy, still they are facing lots of problems that not only affect them but also other people. All though farmers feed the entire nation, sometimes they can't even afford to square meals for themselves and their families.

The world is constantly changing, moving forward at a rapid pace, leaving the ways of the past behind. The agriculture industry is being left in the dust, while machines and technology take over the ways of the world. Being overshadowed by the new ways of life is having a negative impact on the agriculture industry. Urbanization is pushing out the land, factories are compromising the quality of soil, and the working labour pool is getting smaller and smaller.

While these negative things are happening, it's not too late to combat the issues. So far we can reduce the loss of land by setting certain policies and implementing them as gardens in cities. We can set regulation on dumping and engineer new breeds of tolerant plant crops. We can put in place laws that benefit those workers who are willing to pursue a career in the industry. These are just some of the ways we can combat these issues. As we keep advancing, we can advance new ways to fix all these problems, but we have to do it fast. The agriculture industry is one that needs to be preserved in order to sustain life. Without agriculture they would be no food and without food there would be nothing, even no life.

The Indian economy holds the 6th position in the world's top economies. The majority of the country's population depends upon agriculture for their livelihood. Although agricultural sector plays a crucial role in the Indian economy, there is a constant drop in this sector while the service and corporate sectors are comparatively improving.

India's planning prospects also heavily rely on the agricultural sector. A good harvest always offers momentum to the country's projected economic growth by improving the business climate for the transportation system, manufacturing sectors, internal commerce, and so on.

A successful harvest also means that the government will have enough money to cover its budgeted expenditures. Similarly, a bad harvest causes a total depression in the country's business which eventually leads to a collapse of the economy. Thus, does country like India, the agricultural sector place of crucial role, and the Indian economy's prosperity is still heavily reliant on it. As a result, it is clear that agricultural growth is a necessary pre-condition for sectoral diversity and economic development.

The Indian economy is an agro-economy and depends highly on the agricultural sector. Despite just supporting the economy, the agricultural sector also supports the industrial sector and international trade in imports and exports. All though, the contribution of the agricultural sector to the Indian economy is reducing it is the sector with most number of people working in it around the country.

That topic argues that the present global and national legal framework for commercialized seeds and varieties lacks vision in ensuring food security and customer rights for farmers. The mobilization of plant genetic resources is beneficial to plant breeders and large farmers in terms of access to resources and utilization of technology and research. The farmer's freedom to save, share, and re-saw seeds needs to be protected to keep the plant germ plasma alive. Subordination of customary rights of farmers to any exclusive regime that restrains accessibility to, affordable of, and availability of resources for food security and sovereignty. The conclusion proves the argument of erosion of customary rights of farmers during the period of liberalization. In order to establish the statement, an analysis of the economic and legal policy changes against international interference with the Economic rights regime is summarized in this topic.

My concern provides a critical insight into the different factors responsible for indebtedness and feelings of distress among farmers in India. Natural factors like drought, cyclones, and floods, along with institutional factors like inputs, credit, markets, contribute to the capital dependence of farmers. The situations of small, marginal, and large-scale farmers is discussed. After elaborating on the existing conditions, the author suggests measures that could be taken by the government and offers recommendations for overcoming the crisis, such as forming farmers' groups, reducing input costs by adopting non-pesticidal management, rectifying market anomalies, and providing counselling and confidence-building measures in distress hotspots.

The tragedy of farmers committing suicide highlights some of the social and ecological costs linked to the globalization of non-sustainable agriculture. However, these are not crop-specific and have been experienced in all regions where commercially grown and chemically farmed crops are prevalent. Public investments, credit, improvements in infrastructure like roads, transport, and agro-processing stable markets, and knowledge transformation for farmers are the five pillars upon which agrarian prosperity and ruler development can be built. The decent challenge of our times lies in making agriculture a worthwhile and a decent proposition as a livelihood.

As a condition, farmers are either scaling the heights of prosperity or depleting their status. Farmers are sandwiched in between the situations. They are buffeted by lots of **ficlus (page no-222).** We must ponder over their conditions and problems. Our government remains rigid and hardly concerned about farmers and their atrocities.

Scriptures say that as God shuts one door, he opens another. On magnanimity that is similar, even as the government fortifies the Delhi borders for the farmer's march, the government is keeping its mind open on talks with farmers. At this time around, the barricades on the borders are seen to be far deeper and more intimidating than those during the earlier agitation. It is only fair to hope that the government is willing to keep its mind open wider than before. But then why at all the barricades, if the government is confident of its persuasive powers and its avowed concerns for the farmer?

The farmers' demand for guaranteed minimum support prices has remained unanswered for a long time. The talks have failed again and it is strange that the government which acts in many ways, as seen in recent times with the election in mind, has not come forward to accept their legitimate demands. The backbone of the economy in our country is agriculture and the ruling party is very likely to lose a chunk of food from this distressed community if its demands are not met.

Even after a decade in power, it is unfortunate that the Prime Minister and others members in his government still blame the

Congress for deficiencies in governance. The charge this time is that the Congress is dividing people on lines of caste and religion. This should be read in reverse. It is the NDA government, led by BJP that is engineering a divisive policy on caste and religious lines. This is very clear from the time in Parliament that the temple consecration in Ayodhya could usher in a new era that would make generations proud. How will this event solve people's problems? How convenient it is to ignore the burning ethnic issue in Manipur, inflation, and scaling unemployment? If the government has made a record increase in MSP for farmers honour rally tired up on this issue? The opposition is not strong enough to point out the deficiencies in the BJP's policies. People should analyse these issues before voting.

Farmers are being sandwiched between government policies and their demands. The government must take certain steps to help farmers, and mutual understanding is required. Try to demystify complex issues regarding farmer's problems and government concerns. Our country can run smoothly only by joint ventures of farmers and government policies. Both have to ponder intensely about their relationships and contributions. Indian government must pay lead towards farmers' problems and get in return lots of favour and prosperity. So, both join hands and make our country move ahead. Without farmers we can't survive and not even our country. Industrialization and farming are two sides of the same coin. Even industrialization cannot work without agriculture. So, the agricultural sector is really the backbone of our country and economy.

Provide oxygen to formers, provide space to move ahead, and provide opportunities to achieve and then watch them smiling, you and our country. Brick without cement does not build houses, as a country without agriculture will not build strong Nation.

Farmers are our life. They are the real source of energy. So, respect them, adopt them, and help them. No doubt, there are lots of responsibilities but agriculture is above all. We can't help it. It is the world's first profession which entails other professions. This is the base of everything, so do not ignore it. They are everything. They are like the sun, the earth like water, and like air. They are completely an **embodiment** of nature. They are the epitome of nature. So how can we ignore the farmers and the agriculture? Just ponder.

It won't be wrong to say that farmers are the backbone of our Nation and also, they are the driving force behind the Indian economy. Yet all is not well with Indian farmers. They continue to live a life of poverty and misery. Still, they play an important role in nation-building.

Farmers play an extremely important role in any country. They are the people who feed the whole Nation. Let's take a small example to understand the importance of farmers in a better way. When we are hungry, we cannot stay without food. That food reaches our plates only because of farmers. Farmers make a huge contribution to the economy of any country.

The life of farmers is very simple and rooted to the ground. They and their family members who work on the farm wake up early in the morning and spend the whole day in the fields. They plough the land, sow the seeds, water the plants, and do their best to protect the field and the yield. They then wait patiently for the harvest time. Farmer's life is plain and simple. They don't look forward to many luxuries. They look forward to a good harvest and getting a reasonable price for their crops.

Farmer's life in the villages is very different from that of people in cities. Their social life is very different from city folk. They spend all day in the fields. From early morning till sunset, they toil in their fields. The farming activity requires such hard work that they get exhausted when they return home. Their social life is more or less meeting other farmers or people from their neighbourhood post-sundown and sharing their thoughts.

Problems occur with tribal farmers too. The government and other officers try to occupy tribal lands. Government policies stop the struggle farmers from cattle grazing in forest areas or sanctuaries. For example, earlier in the month of February, the notification of the Thanthai Periyar sanctuary in the Erode district of Tamil Nadu triggered conservation among forest dwellers around it. They expressed fear that this is a prelude to their rights under the scheduled tribes and other traditional forest dwellers being denied.

Cattle grazers can no longer graze in the Thanthai Periyar sanctuary. Bargur cattle, a traditional breed native to the Bargur Forest Hills, may now be prevented from accessing their traditional grazing grounds.

Tamil Nadu is not an exception. The same pattern more or less runs across the country. The environment ministry and the forest Bureaucracy continue to defy the laws, Parliament, and the will of the people, leaving forests, forest-dwellers, and wildlife in peril.

Let me come back to farmers' protests or agitation in North India especially around Delhi. Punjab is the major part-taker.

Thousands of farmers started marching on their tractors from Punjab towards Delhi.

Farmers from Punjab have resumed their protest and are trying to come to Delhi just about a month before the 2024 elections are announced. Guaranteed minimum support prices (MSP) are among the key demands being raised by the protesting farmers.

Actually, the conditions of Indian farmers are becoming a matter of concern. Every third Indian farmer was dissatisfied with the prices they received for their output in the market. In terms of quantity, farmers are dissatisfied with a quarter of the disposal of their crop. The dissatisfaction level was much higher among those who grow crops such as fruits, vegetable, pulses, and oil seeds.

This is the critical aspect that farmers' organizations do want to talk about. While there is no denying the fact that large parts of Indian agriculture are facing a viability crisis and a lot of it has to do with not getting remuneration prices for crops, a mindless expansion of MSP operations without a critical look at their existing structure can do more bad than good.

This is the biggest irony in the protest for MSP from Punjab farmers. A large-scale expansion in the cultivation of rice in Punjab- most of it is grown with an eye on MSP- assured procurement- has inflected serious ecological damage to the agricultural ecosystem in this state, leading to severe exploitation of water tables and worsening soil health. A lot of experts have been warning that unless, Punjab moves away from rice cultivation, it could face a serious sustainability crisis as far as the future of farming is concerned in this state.

In an ideal world, the farmers and government, both at the centre and in the state, should have been working together to mitigate this sustainability crisis and use policy as an effective nudge rather than a blanket support or opposition for the demand of a guaranteed MSP.

Delhi is no stranger to protests. As the seat of the national government, the city has seen numerous groups march into Delhi since Independence with demands they believed would be best heard here. From the protest against price rises and authoritarianism in the 1970s to farmers occupying the India Gate Boat Club lawns in the 1980s and Dalits demanding a better life in the 2010s, protesters have taken to the streets of Delhi. In each case, the police and administration have taken measures to avert violence, maintain law and order, and keep disruption to normal life to a minimum.

This is why the response of the administration to the current mobilization of farmer's groups from Punjab seems disproportionate and puzzling. Though the protesters are 200 km away from the capital, the Delhi Police have chosen to virtually shut down the city, seal its borders, blanket it with personnel and barricades that have slowed traffic. They issued random checking of cars and other vehicles to ensure that no farmers were coming in.

This is how the government is treating our farmers. Delhi and Haryana have been converted into garrison. Our farmers are not being allowed to enter Haryana and Delhi. Punjab and Haryana are both brother States since they like different countries by the division of border barricading and lots of other impediments. Are farmers of Punjab not our brothers or they are not citizens of India? The government must allow our farmers to enter Delhi for peaceful protest and let them pass through Haryana. Today, it seems that our country is being divided in different provinces over this issue.

The BJP government is dividing the entire nation and its societies. They are dividing our country and its citizens in the name of caste, creed, religion, profession, ideologies, finance and many more. They are discriminating in everything and in between people even. The situation of farmers is the worst of all. The government is prioritising the business class and the corporate world neglecting farmers and their problems. This is discrimination.

The MSP-based procurement by the FCI has been the bedrock of food security, but the case for its reform is strong. Surplus producers of grain have benefited from the MSP scheme, but the scheme bypasses subsistence farmers in poorer regions. This uneven geographical spread of procurement has also led to unsustainable farm practices in some areas, while farmers in other regions of the country are always on the edge of penury. All this calls for a revamping of the public support for farming, which is essential for reasons that include national food security. This can be achieved better through white political consultation and by encouraging the beneficiaries of the current system to diversify production and increase productivity. The farm sector needs a new model of public support. It cannot be left to the mercy of the market.

But, today drones are being used to fire tear gas shells at the protesting farmers and the placing of formidable barricades that impede their progress are extreme steps. Farmers are not criminals. The government should, on priority, listen to the woes of farmers in all sincerity and seriousness. Let the feeders of the nation be heard. There have been many unfortunate instances of farmers in the recent past. Let the government not hide under the pretext of saying that the agitation is politically motivated.

Agriculture continues to remain an under-invested sector in India. Even farmer are reducing their stakes in agriculture now. This is the most telling statistical predicament of the agriculture sector is concerned. The importance of income from cultivation has fallen significantly for India's agricultural households during this period, and it was not even the largest source of income for agricultural households. An agricultural household is defined as one that produces field or horticultural products, or other specified agricultural products, livestock, etc.

Farmers who diversify their professions and increase their incomes are unlikely to have any incentive to invest in agriculture, even though they still practice it. With both the public and private sectors giving up on long-term investment in agriculture, the future of farming and food security in India is far from secure.

Due to farmers' protests, the cities bordering Haryana and Uttar Pradesh are very barricaded and fortified with concrete blocks, containers, and barber wires, the police dug trenches on the streets and bylanes at the Singhu Border to prevent the protesting farmers from entering Delhi.

I condemn the Haryana government for unprovoked police action against protesting farmers. The Haryana BJP government has no right to stop farmers who are peacefully heading to Delhi to hold protests. Delhi is the capital of our country; anyone can enter Delhi without any restrictions. Then why our farmers are not allowed? The National Highway is the property of nation and farmers are just going to pass from Haryana's jurisdiction to reach

Delhi. I consider the action of the government unconstitutional and illegal.

Protesting farmers begin receiving support from several like-minded groups across the country. Government must desist from such attacks on democratic right to protest. The late M.S. Swaminathan's daughter, economist Madhura Swaminathan, during a speech made at the Indian agricultural Research Institute, urged the centre to not to treat farmers as criminals. Such kind of atrocities that are being meted out to farmers, the barbaric suppression, should be stopped immediately. There valid demand of MSP, for which they were given an assurance, needs to be fulfilled. If the BJP government tries to go back on its word, the government will not succeed.

Prime Minister Narendra Modi has 'betrayed' farmers by not implementing the Swaminathan Commission's recommendation on minimum support price (MSP) and should apologize to the country and the farmers for it.

Look at the plight of our farmers —how their voices are being silenced by the government. Their demands are being trampled by the merciless feet of government. In spite of listening, or even helping the farmers, the government is behaving very rudely with them. I predict that one day the government will face the consequences. God will listen to farmers. The day is not so far, when farmers will carry the day.

Is it a democracy or dictatorship in our country? There is, I think dictatorship in disguise. The present-day situation in our country seems that democracy is lacking far behind. Our country will face dire consequences in the future, if the situation is not controlled.

As described earlier, farmers are the backbone of our economy. So, we cannot bypass the importance of the farmers and agriculture. Actually, our government is paying lead towards industrialisation and private sectors in isnpiteof the basic realities. Without farmers, even industrialisation and private sector cannot to prevail. No existence of anything without agriculture. Farmer create base for everything. Raw material and scores of requirements are being by the farmers. The person who is providing everything to the nation is deprived of his right and his share. Our country needs to ponder over the situation of farmers and agriculture and step ahead with positive results.

Today's government is dividing our country and society in different segments, and it will entail disaster. Party benefits and favours can create chaos in our country. Think about it deeply. No farmers, no food and no economy. They are God and you are challenging God. The government is blindfolded part 1 they will be realize from blindfold they will they will find a score of difficulties and chaos.

It is my humble request to all, to support our farmers. I plead my central government to support farmers and listen their issues. Shake hands with farmers, and you will realize the strength of our nation. Farmers are embodiment of God, so respect them. If you are ignoring them, you will be in big trouble. Our country will be in big trouble. Farming and industrialisation is both side of the same coin.

One often repeated shibboleth is, "farmers are the backbone of our country," appears to have lost its importance given the stance of the government at the center. One wonders whether this second stir by the farmers will have the desired effect. Madhura

Swaminathan has a point in requesting the center not to treat the farmers as criminals. But is anyone hearing this appeal?

The traditional weed-paddy cycle is no longer remunerative and has also dried up groundwater resources. It has now reached a stage where substantial increases in production have become uneconomic and unsustainable for these crops despite assured MSP procurement. The imperative need is to change current practices with new technology to ensure sustainability. It is not about farmers being obstinate but about the government having to give farmers new packages.

Farmer's stagnant incomes and the pain that labourers face pertaining to the loss may need to be deliberated threadbare. Everyone involved must show sagacity, leaving no transfer fragile situations to go down this slippery slope. The contours of welfare must be kept in mind.

The ongoing protest underscores the need for comprehensive agricultural reforms. While demanding MSP, farmers' welfare are crucial, there is a necessity to address regional disparity in procurement and promote sustainable farming practices. The government must engage in inclusive political discussions to revamp public support for agriculture, ensuring a balanced and resilient system beyond market uncertainties.

Actually, the farmers demanding a legal guarantee for minimum support prices (MSP) have been discussed. The farmers asserted that the meeting would be fruitful only if the government came out with something positive to offer. Haryana is using force against the farmers, injuring many of them. Haryana Chief Minister Manohar Lal Khattar objected to farmer's approach in pressing for the fulfilment of their demands. It is because, in Haryana, its BJP let the government. BJP is trying to crush the agitation of farmers by all means. Anti-farmer government. And act must be made on MSP as guarantee.

Respected government, do not bardon, be practical, and pass the bill on MSP. Actually your words do not keep any value, so finalize it by approving MSP legally. False promises often made out the time of elections are absolutely null and void. Many a slip in between cup and lips. Farmers are crusaders for a cause that touches my heart. God only knows when a farmer's financial uncertainty is likely to dissipate soon. A little effort on the part of the government will go a long way in mending fences with farmers. Transparency in negotiations can remove all apprehension in going ahead with a deal.

The Nation's economic woes stem from the Modi regime's staggering incompetence. It has been unable to put together a well-thought-out, cohesive economic philosophy. The government is obsessed with untrammeled power to do as it pleases. Democracy is a nuisance. Consequently, fear is a hard and visible reality today, never since the emergency of 1975 -77 has there been so much fear in society. My conclusion is blunt and brutal. " our democracy is in crisis, our social fabric is torn, our economy is in peril."

As I have mentioned earlier farmers and agriculture are our backbone. Our government policies are trying to injure this backbone. Once the backbone is injured, our economy and country will not be able to stand. They will be crawling. We will find ourselves and our nation in the ambit of darkness and distress. It is my humble request to my government to cope with such kind of problems by hugging our farmers. Farmers are gentle by nature. Once, you listen to their problems and help them, they can shut their blood for the nation as they always do.

Let me explain the importance of farmers and their contributions to our system. Farmers are like the roots of a tree. The tree is our country. The stem of the tree resembles the Government and the branches are our administration, and last but not least, the leaves, fruits, and flowers are public. So if farmers are strong enough, the tree of the nation will flourish for a long. If the roots are strong, the stem will stand still, and if the stem is strong, the tree will bear fruits. Same with the country. So, try to think deeply about roots mean about the farmers. They are the lifeline of our nation. Do not try to cut this line, otherwise we will fall and die. Think over it.

On the eve of the crucial meeting with the center, protesting farmers from Punjab, camped at different locations along the boundary with Haryana. Farmers ask the union government to bring an ordnance for a legal guarantee to minimum support price (MSP) for crops.

At Shambhu addressing a press conference, Sardar Sarvan Singh Pandher of the Kisan Majdoor Morcha (KMM) said that the government should immediately issue the ordnance if it wants to resolve the farmers' protest. If the Modi government's intent is clear towards resolving the issue, then they can bring an ordnance on legal guarantee for MSP immediately.

In Haryana, farmers associated with the Bhartiya Kisan Union took out a tractor march at several places including Kurukshetra, Yamunanagar, and Sirsa to extend support to the demands and their farmer brothers from Punjab. A Mahapanchayat was held at Kurukshetra to devise a strategy for extending support to the farmers.

Himachal Pradesh's Chief Minister, Sukhwinder Singh Sukhu, presented the tax-free budget, with a focus on the rural economy.

Mr. Sukhu, who holds the finance portfolio too, presented the state budget in favour of state citizens and farmers.

Calling agriculture the 'backbone' of the state's economy, Mr. Sukhu also announced in new 'Rajiv Gandhi prakartik kheti start-up Yojana' scheme, aimed at increasing the income of the farmers in the state. Under this scheme, in the first phase, 10 farmers from each panchayat will be encouraged to undertake chemical-free farming. The government will purchase their grain at the minimum support price (MSP).

The chief minister, Mr. Sukhu, in a dig at the BJP, alleged that the Himachal government did not receive any special relief package from the center despite the unprecedented natural disaster during the last monsoon season, which saw heavy floods.

Due to wrong politics and policies in the past, total liabilities in the form of loans have risen. However, the present BJP government did not allow the place of development to slow down due to a lack of resources. Such discrimination among the states within our country because of BJP government. Shame!

The recent rise in the cotton price in the international market and of cotton sold by the Cotton Corporation of India (CCI) in the domestic market has become a matter of concern to textile mills, especially small-scale units.

Current Indian cotton prices are lower than the international prices by almost rupees 4000 and the association expect cotton exports this season to be almost 20 lakh bales.

Around 65% of the Indian crop (about 200 bales) has arrived in the market and the domestic demand is very good. A few people have increased the prices when they bid for cotton sold by the Cotton Corporation of India.

The textile industry is grappling with poor international demand and domestic sales, and the impact of finished garments has intensified competition. It is worth noting that the (RBI) Reserve Bureau of India has rated the textile industry as 'Red', further highlighting the severity of the situation.

What does it show? Such kind of data tries to describe that farmers of cotton are minting money and are flourishing as their prosperity is concerned. I say not at all. These farmers are facing scores of problems regarding sustainable prices. Farmers in Maharashtra are committing suicide. Why? It is all **gimmicks**. And if it is so, according to the textile industry, why do they get disturbed or perturbed by the prices? The same goes for farmers. Such kinds of data and reports try to fool the people. They are ignoring and by passing the ground realities.

Farmers are farmers; whether they are of grains, vegetables, fishing, horticulture, cotton, and spices. All these face lots of atrocities in their lives. They are simple and down to earth. They are always being fooled by different government policies. They feed us but they are hungry. Look at the irony of Fate, that the creator of food empty stomach. May God help them!

Farmers were being exploited and oppressed in different ways under the Kurki and Jeenkathiya systems. The Neeley British planters had confiscated more than 1 lakh acres of fertile land and set up their house there. The farmers raised their voices against the atrocities, and forced them to abolish the system through Satyagraha.

The Union Minister of Agriculture and Farmers Welfare, Shri Radha Mohan Singh said that there is no other example in human Civilization of the war based by the farmers in a peaceful way against the operation and injustice of the British under the leadership of Gandhiji.

The same is happening today. The innocent disarmed farmers raise their voices against the atrocities, exploitation, oppression, and extortion of the government and force them to abolish the system. Today's government used to pay some money to the farmers by mortgaging their land and houses and compiling them to sow Indigo.

The backbone of our nation, Indian farmers do not have easy lives. They have conducted several farmer movements in India that have become a vital part of Indian history.

India has a rather long history of the farmer movement that has shaped their social and economic conditions to a large extent today. Its origin can be traced back to the colonial era when farmers from across the country mobilized in large numbers to protest against the atrocities perpetrated against them. They revolted against issues like high tax regimes, blatant exploitation, underpayment against them, and losing rights over their land.

India was a largely agrarian society when the British occupied the country. Agriculture was not conducted without its problems but it was sufficient for the sustainability and livelihood of farmers. However, the British wanted to maximize their own profit at the expense of farmers and peasants. During the colonial era, farmers had to go through problems like:

1. The exploitation of agricultural labours. Zamindars and landlords exploit poor farmers to the points that many even worked as bonded labours. Their wages were abysmally low, their working hours were terribly long, and they were deprived of basic dignity.

2. The colonial rules carefully devised policies that benefited those who are already privileged. They were men to protect and benefit money lenders and landlords.

3. Tax rates during colonial Era one of the highest in the world. Even if the farmers' crops failed, they were not exempted from paying taxes. Many sold their children and made their wives assessable to the British just to keep up with the tax.

4. It was major impediment to farmers' economic conditions and growth. It was prevalent mostly in the Bengal Presidency. Under this system, whatever profits were made on the farm went to the zamindar's pockets instead of farmers.

Farmer movements in the country before 1900's were u norganised and staggered. Farmer's movement in India after the 1900s play the huge role in the overall Nationalist movement. For peasants were made aware of their rights and their role in the freedom struggle. They struggled against the unfair tax regimes and policies imposed by the British government. Through non-corporation and non-violence, they brought the British to their knees, emerging out victorious in the end.

The same situation is going on with farmers in present India. The government is repeating the blunder mistake regarding farmers and agriculture. They are bypassing the agriculture sector, and they will face the music in future. You are Indians, not British, so think positively about our agriculture sector and farmers.

It's our duty and responsibility to keep our farmers along with us in the journey of progress and development. There should be proper nexus in between agriculture and industrialisation. They are strong hands of our nation. Let them both make the pace of equality and contribution. Peace and duties are the same side of the same coin. Government is to lead us and farmers are to feed us.

Farmers are the lifeline of the economy. Don't try to neglect them. They are source of life . Do not disparge them, hey are our lives. Don't forget their contributions in the gleaming situation is in perit. They do a lot and received nothing. Such an irony of fate?

Farmers do not want a lot. They just demand their actual cost of their sweat. They are the foundation of our economy. If, someone is going to dismantle the foundation, the edifice our country will fall and we will be crushed.

Every business and industrialisation projects from farming and agriculture. For their survival they have to accept the importance of agriculture. Without agriculture they cannot survive. Agriculture is lifeline to the industrialisation. Then on what platform and reasoning, you are ignoring farmers and agriculture. This is what like, you are copulating your wife and expecting good result as a child. But, if you are not feeding her properly and not making her happy accordingly, you will get opposite your desire, even nothing. Same with the farmers and agriculture. So, respect the farmers and prostrate in front of agriculture.

Farmers in certain parts of the country are restive once again. They have started marching towards Delhi to exert pressure on the union government through sittings. They claimed the government has not kept the promise it made to them.

Agriculture in India needs a new vision and strategy, and not just at ad hoc interventions. It will now have to adapt to changing circumstances. Agriculture has shaped or society and culture for centuries, but farmers have always been under stress. They continue to worry over the decreasing size of land holdings, increasing water scarcity, and land becoming progressively infertile. Has the government under blind eye to their problems, forcing them to obstruct road and railway traffic?

In the 2019 interim budget, the union government resolved to grand farming households 6,000 INR each year from the treasury. Similarly, during the covid-19 pandemic, the government begin providing free food grain and edible oil every month to the needy.

These schemes have since continued and are regarded as a great aid in the villages of Uttar Pradesh, Uttarakhand and Bihar. The central and state government also separate numerous social programs for children of farmers and agriculture labours and for women involved in farming. The needy benefit from direct cash transfer to farmer account. Not just that, this class is also entitled to several other agricultural concessions. It does not require any great inside to discern the positive impact these have had on the rural economy.

If this is the case, why are farmers' and farm workers' suicide rates climbing year after year?

According to National Crime Records Bureau (NCRB) data, 11,290 people associated with agriculture died by suicide in 2022. Of these, 5,027 were farmers, while 6,083 worked on farms as labourers. This year such deaths have grown by 3.75%

over last year. These are worrying figures, to be sure, but not everyone who is experiencing bad luck is associated with agriculture. In data from 2022, 170,921 suicides were reported to the NCRB. Of these, 11.6% for self-employed, 11.6% were housewives, 9.6% were unemployed, 9.2% were employed and 7.6% were students. Another 26% were daily wage workers. Farmer ranked 7th on this list.

But a suicide is a suicide. The entire social and economic system must be held accountable for this. The solution takes resources, time, and patience.

Another issue also needs to be discussed here. It is commonly stated that the agriculture sector contributed more than half of India's Gross Domestic Product (GDP) when the country gained independence in 1947. In 2022-23, this becomes just 15%. This figure is sometimes presented as a reflection of the deteriorating situation in agriculture, despite the fact that in rapidly developing countries, industry, trade, and service sectors are expanding significantly.

Are the demands made by the protesting farmers unjustified? No. They have their own grief and suffering. We have to look at these. But it is impossible to overlook the fact that other sections of the population also require government assistance just as much, if not more, as the figures here make evident.

Before the 1970s, India was not self-sufficient in producing food grains and imported a large sum of food grains from other countries. But, when our imports started blackmailing us then Prime Minister Lal Bahadur Shastri found an alternative and motivated our farmers in addition, he gave the slogan " Jai Jawan Jai Kisan" which is remembered till day.

Farmers and agriculture are the base of our economy. We can't neglect them and their contribution. They are like supporting devices. Once, the device is removed we will die. Our standing poster is due to agriculture. Oxygen, materials, vitamins, and not many more we grab from agriculture. Agriculture is our first and initial source of life. Kindly pay lead towards agriculture and figures. Without them, we are null and void.

No doubt farmers are moving ahead but by education and services land holdings are decimated to null and void. Education is essential for everyone, especially farmers. But how many farmers are educated? Today, only 10 to 20% of farmers are educated, rest face problems.

Farmers are the oxygen we breathe in. A farmer is a person who runs and works on a farm. Some farmers raise a variety of food crops, while others keep Dairy cows, and buffaloes and sell their milk. Farmers work in some aspect of agriculture, growing vegetables, grains, and fruits are raising animals for milk, eggs, meat, and many more. Think, without farmers, we can't fill our bellies. They are feeders and we are consumers. We and our entire country are at the stake of agriculture.

Now, I am concluding my ideas regarding agriculture and farmers. The agriculture sector is of vital importance for the region. It is undergoing a process of transition to a market economy, with substantial changes in the social, legal, structural productivity and supply, as is the case with all other sectors of the economy.

The world is constantly changing, moving forward at a rapid pace, leaving the ways of the past behind. The agriculture industry is being left in the dust, while machines and technology take over the ways of the world. Being overshadowed by the new ways of life is having a negative impact on the agriculture industry. Urbanization is pushing out the land, factories are compromising the quality of soil, and the working labour pool is getting smaller in smaller.

While all these negative things are happening, it's not too late to combat the issues. So far we can reduce the loss of land by setting policies and implementing it as a garden in cities. We can set regulations on dumping and engineer new breeds of tolerant plant crops. We can put in place laws that benefit those workers who are willing to pursue a career in the industry.

These are just some of the ways we can combat the issues. As we keep advancing, we can advance new ways to fix all these problems, but we have to do it fast. The agriculture industry is one that needs to be preserved in order to sustain life. Without agriculture, there would be no food, and without food, there would be nothing.

Agriculture is an integral part of smart growth. The ability to feed one's own population is critical to the independence of any state. Ontario is blessed with resources that have facilitated the development of a world-class agriculture industry that provides safe, nutritious, and reliable food. The ability to feed the local population from local sources should not underestimated.

Agriculture is a diverse industry with very specific locational connections. Certain crops can only be grown in specific locations where the combination of a variety of factors including soil, moisture, temperature, and topography is right. When such areas are lost to agriculture, the ability to produce crops that require a particular combination of factors is also lost. The public needs to understand that agricultural land is a non-renewable resource requiring appropriate management techniques. Before allowing it to go out of production, decision-makers must consider the implications of that decision and evaluate it in terms of the long-term loss to Ontario.

This will not be an easy task; forecasting is never easy. The agricultural industry has advanced greatly in the past few decades.

Agricultural policies must be flexible enough to accommodate further changes.

For the agriculture community, uncertainty is a major issue. Farmers are used to dealing with uncertainty related to weather, they expect it and are prepared for it. What they do not expect and cannot deal with is ongoing economic uncertainty. Uncertainty related to legislative context within which they must work uncertainly about land use controls or environmental regulation. The **pervasive pessimism** among even the most successful farmers needs to be addressed. The average of farmers is rising and the pessimistic attitude discourages triangle generation from entering the sector.

Regulation of this sector is often rigid. Traditionally, issues have been compartmentalized and dealt with individually. This is the antithesis of what a successful form operation requires, where issues are interrelated and need to be considered together. Rigid regulations that are slow to change preclude the flexibility the industry needs to be successful. To preserve agriculture, it is not enough to preserve the land. Society must also preserve the farmer. For this to happen, farmers must operate in an environment where they are certain of the rules and can respond quickly to changing local, national, and international markets.

Farmers face lots of atrocities in their lives. They provide everything and receive nothing or less. Imagine, if farmers are not there or an agricultural is not there, what will happen? Just think! The world will be without food. So, respect farmers and invigorate the agriculture by all means.

Agriculture is the first and initial industry in the world. Agriculture projects all other businesses and industrialization. Agriculture is base of everything. Agriculture is life. Agriculture and farmers are the lifeline of the world and entire humanity. The strength of farmers is like the flow of the river. If you are devoting the holy river and bathing with all rituals, it will bless you, or otherwise, if you challenge its nature, it will flush you far away and your life will end. Same with the agriculture and farmers. If we stick against farmers and agriculture, we will get hurt and finished. So, consider farmers like God and respect them. Agriculture and farmers are the real assets of our country.

We can't ignore agriculture and the importance of farmers. They project the importance, and reflect the result of our economy. The graph of the economy is always upgraded due to agriculture. At the time of lockdown due to covid.

This will not be an easy task, for forecasting is never easy. The agricultural industry has advanced greatly in the past few decades.

So, agriculture and farmers are our real strengths. They feed everyone on earth. Along with human beings, they feed animals and birds as well. They are very kind-hearted and strong.

It would not be wrong to say, that farmers are the backbone of our nation and also, they are the driving force behind the Indian economy. Yet all is not well with Indian farmers. They continue to live a life of poverty and misery. Still, they play and important role in nation-building.

As mentioned earlier, farmers are the backbone of the Indian economy. More than half of the Indian population relies on agriculture as a source of income. Farmers not only make the country secure by providing food, fodder, and other raw materials as food stock for industries, but they also serve as a source of livelihood for the majority of the Indian population. Sadly, though farmers feed the entire population, they sometimes sleep without having the right meals.

Farmers are the soul of the nation. Agriculture is the only means of living for almost two-thirds of the employed class in India. Farmers produce crops, pulses, and vegetables which are needed by everyone. They work extremely hard, so we can have food on our table every day. So, whenever we have a meal or eat food, we must thank the farmer.

Farmers are also involved in other small businesses such as dairy, meat, poultry, fisheries, food grains etc. India has also emerged as the second-largest producer of fruits and vegetables in the world.

Farmers face various issues and challenges related to agriculture. Some of them are poorly maintained irrigation systems and a lack of good extension services. Farmer's excess to market is hampered by poor roads, rudimentary market infrastructure, and excessive regulation. Our country has inadequate infrastructure and services for farmers because of low investment. Most of the farmers hold small areas of land due to which they are restricted to use traditional methods of farming.

If small farmers want to increase their production, they have to use good-quality seeds, proper irrigation systems, advanced farming tools and techniques, pesticides, fertilizers, etc. For all this, they need money, due to which they have no choice but to take debt or loans from banks. They have immense pressure to produce crops so as to yield profit. In case, then their crops fail, all their efforts go in vain. In fact, then they are not able to produce enough to even fill the stomachs of their families.

Change is happening in rural India but it still has a long way to go. Farmers have benefited from improved farming techniques, but the growth is not equitable. The efforts should be to stop the migration of farmers to urban areas. To make agriculture successful and profitable, it is vital that proper thrust be given to the improvement of the condition of marginal and small farmers.

Now I am going to conclude myself on the lot topic of farmers and their atrocities. We must pay the lead towards farmers and the agriculture sector deeply. Government must listen to farmer's problems and try to solve them. I have tried to demystify this topic and the subject of farmers and agriculture in a simple way.

'Farming and agriculture are the foundation of every economics structure.'